a Memoir

Nandi Sojourner Crosby

.

Nandi Sojourner Crosby, Ph.D.
Department of Sociology
California State University, Chico
Chico, CA 95929-0445

ISBN: 979-8-9885911-0-8 (Paperback)
ISBN: 979-8-9885911-1-5 (Hardcover)

This book is a memoir. It reflects the author's present recollections of experiences over time. Many names have been changed, a few events have been compressed, and some dialogue has been paraphrased for clarity.

Cover Art: Jason O'Brien

First Print Edition: 2023
Second Print Edition: 2025

"Found in Translation."

Jason O'Brien, the Canadian painter of my cover art explains this piece as a woman who represents many transitions and realities at different stages in her life. With each significant experience, she has survived and regained a sense of self. She is observed through various stages of her life, constantly adapting to challenges, setbacks, and hardships. Despite losing parts of herself along the way, she rebuilds and discovers new aspects that reflect her will, strength, and resilience. Between the unforeseen ups and downs of life, she undergoes a transformation. Evolving through personal and spiritual growth, she ultimately realizes that even though her life may not have had the outcome she intended, she has discovered the person she needed to become.

jasonobriengallery.com

Contents

ACKNOWLEDGMENTS

Writing this book has been one of the most challenging and rewarding journeys of my life, and I could not have reached this point without the unwavering support of so many remarkable people. To my husband, T. LaMichael Williams—your endless patience and love carried me through every rough draft and moment of doubt. Your quiet strength and willingness to listen, even when the words were messy and incomplete, gave me the courage to keep going. Having you beside me has been a gift beyond measure. All of me loves all of you.

To the current and former prisoners who opened their lives and hearts to me—you transformed more than this book. You transformed me. I am forever grateful for the lessons you shared and the trust you placed in me to tell these stories.

To my beloved mother, Sandra, and my devoted aunt Shelia—your love has been my anchor and my refuge. And to my uncle Earl, thank you for nurturing my endless curiosity and inspiring the path that led me here. My friends and family, your steady encouragement was the light I needed on the darkest days.

To my students and colleagues at Chico State and Butte College, thank you for creating spaces that challenge and inspire me. Your ideas and energy fueled this work in ways you may never know. To Mercedes and Khadijah, your thoughtful editorial guidance was invaluable—I am so lucky to have had your eyes and minds on these pages.

And to you, the reader—thank you for opening this book and stepping into these stories with me. Your willingness to engage with this work makes it all worthwhile. I hope these pages offer you moments of reflection, compassion, and a deeper understanding of our shared humanity.

From the depths of my heart, thank you.

FOREWORD

Written by Joe

Prison is a dehumanizing, concentrated mockery of life. I know this because I confront the reality of this monster consuming my humanity—daily. Many of you probably think of prison as simply a place where criminals are held as punishment. Prison is also the embodiment of dangerous ideas about the human condition and the worth of human beings.

Most of you, thankfully, have never experienced the psychological and emotional isolation that I, and millions of prisoners throughout the United States, experience as an inherent part of our daily lives. Statistically, at least some of you know someone, a family member or friend, who is doing time. Many more of you know someone who has a family member or friend in prison. Prison touches all our lives directly or indirectly. It has become a part of our collective reality.

As the days turn into weeks, then into months, years, and decades, everything I have relied upon to remind myself that I am real—that I am a human worthy of love, of being cared for, of caring about another human more than I care about myself—have slowly disappeared from my life. My communications with acquaintances, both old and new, are sufficiently strained by the realities of the hyper-control imposed upon me. My imprisonment is now more than a decade in the making. Time drowns my voice and silences my pleas for support. The acquaintances who have endured have become lost outside the concrete box in which I have not only been exiled but entombed. On rare occasions when my voice has found itself strong enough to permeate such limitations, it carries with it the foul odor of my wasted life in this degenerated place. As the years go by, friends and family move on with their lives, accepting the void I have left. Inevitably, my presence will completely vanish from their memories, and I, too, will be alone in utter isolation to confront the madness that is prison; this is part of our collective experience.

What saddens me most is that there are hundreds of thousands of prisoners experiencing this aloneness, experiencing their own disappearance. Time collapses upon us, and nothing else exists except the here and now. Our only connection to anything other than the perpetual antagonism of our imprisonment is the people with whom we interact, who keep our presence with them in letters and an occasional visit, which represents both financial and emotional hardships for us all. Those loved ones are our only connection to the free world. They are our connection to things that remind us of what it means to be alive, to be truly human.

Long periods of imprisonment at this depth of emotional and social isolation, which is the absolute reduction of our existence in the mundane and trivial rituals of incarceration, are not conducive to even a semblance of a meaningful life. All our insecurities and the trauma of our lives remind us of things that are wrong with us and how we were never good enough. These things about ourselves explain why friends and family leave us alone here to suffer. We blame ourselves and resent the world for reminding us of our failures.

Anger and frustration at ourselves become all-consuming, and we find strength and the will to face another day in that anger and frustration. The extreme antagonism provides meaning to our suffering because in the end, it is all we have. It drives all our interactions and defines many of our experiences here. It injects itself into our interactions with other prisoners, guards, and relationships with our loved ones.

§

I met Nandi during her solo tour of the prison facility where I was housed in northern California. Since that first encounter, I have learned a lot about Nandi. While our interactions were sometimes reducible to a few passages of roughly scribed words strewn on the backs and fronts of paper, our deep connection has brought a painful awareness of those things about which I am insecure and woefully inadequate.

However, our connection has also spawned my creativity, growth, and desire to be more than I am. It encourages me to nurture the emotionally mature human being I am becoming. Nandi has touched my life. She has helped me realize not just who I am. She has inspired me to be more than Prisoner #P70334.

The book you hold is Nandi's testimony of how those of us behind the walls of one prison or another who have been fortunate enough to encounter her engaging soul through correspondence or in person, have influenced her life. Undoubtedly, we have imposed upon her consciousness and understanding of where we are, who we are, and who we desperately want to become. We have shown her the human cost of mass incarceration. This book is a testament to the very thing that is relentlessly devoured by the beast of our imprisonment—our humanity—and her own.

To be free is not merely to cast off one's chains, but to live in a way that respects and enhances the freedom of others.

Nelson Mandela

THE PRISONERS I ONCE LOVED

To forgive is to set a prisoner free and discover
the prisoner was you.

Lewis B. Smedes

I was 19 years old the first time I wrote to a prisoner. He
posted an ad in the newspaper, and I was enthralled. We had
been pen pals for a year when I drove hundreds of miles from
my college campus in Maryland to meet him in North
Carolina. Reggie had just been transferred to a pre-release
facility that allowed him to work as a barber outside the
prison during the day. His supervisor covered for him, and
we spent the afternoon together. The year was 1989.

Despite promises to be lifelong friends, Reggie and I lost

contact following his release two months after our meeting. Our experience was positive, and I craved more of that sort; thus, I continued to reach out to prisoners over the years. Now, I can reflect on decades of writing letters, visiting, emailing, befriending, and even loving countless incarcerated and formerly incarcerated people. The relationships have been incredible and have shaped me into a different person despite the challenges and occasional pain they brought.

This book highlights some of my encounters with prisoners across the country, the meaningful experiences we shared, and our profound impact on each other. A couple of the relationships I detail here began in the early 1990s when I was in my 20s. Now in my mid-50s, several connections are newer, and the feelings are still raw. My curiosity about imprisoned people and prison culture led me to travel from one coast to the other at least ten times, accept thousands of calls, write countless letters, offer kindness, share secrets, spend unfathomable amounts of money, and open my home to people with rap sheets pages long.

I could not have imagined the profound impact prison and prisoners would have on me. As I look back on my journey, I am filled with gratitude and hope. I am grateful for the opportunity to have walked alongside these women and men and witnessed their strength, resilience, and humanity. I hope their stories will inspire others to see the potential for redemption and change in all of us. Each person I've known has taught me something valuable about the human condition. I've seen how love, compassion, and understanding can make a difference in someone's life. And I've witnessed the power of redemption. This experience has reaffirmed my belief in the goodness of humanity. Alas, this journey has also taught me that humans have the capacity to do horrible, unfathomable things.

My wide range of encounters with prisoners has included conflict, friendship, love, and heartbreak. The chapters in this book lay those experiences bare. While all the chapters describe crimes they committed, the essence of the story lies in the dynamics of our connection and how their pre-, post-, or current carceral status was a critical factor in how we showed up to each other. We fiercely debated political issues, triggered childhood traumas, supported and celebrated our accomplishments, and discussed our visions of social justice. Occasionally, we connected after years of not speaking. Other times, we let go forever. It is unlikely that I will meet most of the people in this book again.

§

I once had a prison friendship with a man named Dante. He was in his tenth year of being locked up for bank robbery when I twice traveled to South Carolina from my home in California to visit with him. After being friends with him for a year, his mother passed away alone in her Washington, D.C., apartment. Soon after her body was discovered, Dante received a request from the city to provide an address to forward her ashes. He asked me to keep them until his release.

"Of course," I replied, glad to be of assistance.

After a few weeks, I received a standard post office box containing a clear Ziploc bag filled with bone fragments and ashes. Four years later, just days after his release, I flew to D.C. and delivered his mother's ashes to him. We remain friendly on social media.

Like my connection with Dante, I have had strong ties to prisoners but chose not to dedicate a full chapter to them.

Most are not featured because the nature of our relationship, like the one I had with Dante, is captured in the stories I do share in Prisoners I Once Loved. Thus, devoting additional chapters would essentially repeat the same narrative about generosity, separation, kindness, and loss.

Also, some relationships I formed with inmates were relatively superficial. We may have exchanged a handful of letters, but our affiliation failed to develop substance. Paris is one such person. I first learned of her when I viewed a documentary about Maryland's only women's prison. Paris stated that she refused to accept that she would be incarcerated forever, despite being guilty of shooting a teenager who she believed talked to the cops about her drug dealing and being sentenced to life without parole. Where are you going, Ms. Lady? Most of our conversations were about our dating lives, in which she frequently gave me unsolicited advice. I often nudged her to stop using offensive language to refer to women's bodies. We both agreed to make better choices. Paris asked me to send her magazine subscriptions. I did. We stopped writing for no apparent reason after exchanging less than a dozen letters,

I decided to remove four chapters at the eleventh hour due to concerns about the quality of my own writing. I became bored reading them. One of those chapters was about my work with the Incarcerated Students Program, where I taught college classes to women and men imprisoned throughout California. The story reads more like a rant about teaching courses only through correspondence rather than face-to-face. I was sure no one wanted to read about my disdain for grading stacks of papers with assignments that required imprisoned students to merely answer the questions at the end of each chapter of a textbook. I want to be in the classroom with them. Instead of boring you with that dream, I deleted that essay from this manuscript and poured out a special libation for the ancestors to make things happen for me.

Drafting this manuscript required immense courage because it meant reliving harrowing experiences and exposing myself. So why do it? Words are powerful. They swirl around my head all day, every day, but they become magic once I write them down. I think of my life as a series of stories that allow me to examine people, contexts, choices, and outcomes that show me how I arrived at the place where I am today—curious about, engaged in, and alive with prisoners as a core feature of my identity.

Every chapter highlights a unique story of connection, love, and loss. "During the 2 a.m. Hour," the first story, delves into the life of my cousin Shawn, with whom I shared a close bond in our childhood. Regrettably, Shawn's home life was marred by abuse, which led to years of crime, addiction, and multiple incarcerations.

"Goodbye to Yesterday" highlights my employment as a correctional officer in a maximum-security prison in 1992, just before my 23rd birthday. Assigned to Maryland's newest maximum-security men's prison, I faced challenges while learning the ropes of the job.

"More Human than Legend" updates a story from my earlier memoir. In this chapter, I recount my interactions with a notorious figure from my neighborhood in Baltimore whose larger-than-life reputation converged in encounters many years after I first heard his name.

Two chapters center around sex offenders and the turmoil I experienced. The first is titled "nadir," a man I allowed into my life and home, unaware of why he was incarcerated. I do not capitalize his name because the everyday version of the word is a more incredible testament to my experience of him than the proper noun he chose as his name. The second, "Sex Offender Hell," is about a man trying to end the sex offender registry. The nature of their crimes is central to how I experienced them and key to the stories I present here.

Multiple chapters showcase my engagement with pen pals I created after seeing them in a documentary. I developed a remarkable friendship with Halim, who was convicted at 16 years old. The story "Flowers Grow in Winter" highlights how we inspired each other to mature. Justin, the focus of "The Human Cost" chapter, was featured in a National Geographic documentary. He gave me a slight sense of how long-term solitary confinement changes people. After years of being alone, he and others have developed mental health issues that make it almost impossible to live in the free world again.

In the chapters "Foot Solder" and "In the Stars," I invite readers to witness relationships with men who are former white supremacist gang members. For one of them, I offered him more support than I do for most people. I connected with the other one online. Their past involvement in promoting racist ideas did not impact our relationship.

Alongside my friendships with imprisoned people, I have volunteered in both women's and men's prisons. "When They Speak About Their Children" highlights a couple of experiences I had over eleven years of volunteering in one prison. "O.G. J" focuses on a man who attended a workshop I facilitated at an Atlanta prison and later became a close friend. In the chapter "Johnny & JDP," I encountered men who shared stories of regret, remorse, and personal growth, intending to inspire young people to make positive choices. Though distinct, "Bittersweet" and "Love is the Only Freedom" center around the theme of love.

Throughout my life, I have developed romantic feelings for imprisoned men. In fact, I even chose to marry one. I share this story in "Losing the First 200 Pounds is the Hardest." Although our relationship was short-lived, I became a different person after the impact he left. Therefore, the chapter dedicated to our relationship is lengthy, as it is a pivotal relationship that shaped my approach to life, love, and self-worth. To grasp the profound effects of that relationship, it is necessary to explore my journey through the preceding chapters. Only then, in the final chapter about my marriage, can one truly understand the significance of all the prisoners I once loved.

§

This book is an authentic, firsthand account of relationships that taught me invaluable lessons and allowed me to express compassion and love in ways that made the most sense to me. I had never thought of all the relationships I developed with current and former prisoners as a tapestry with myself as the common thread. Every word I wrote reveals patterns and insights into my thoughts, and I learned a great deal about myself in the process. I now know there were moments when I may have been too quick to offer support, overlooked certain cautionary signs, or held on for longer than I should have.

Conversely, I took pride in being a reliable friend, an empathetic listener, and a source of support. I let my guard down when necessary and held my ground when it counted—but sometimes, I confused the two. As the tapestry expanded, so did my understanding of the complex and nuanced experience of being fully human.

Writing allowed me to reflect on my past, embrace hard truths, and acknowledge my growth. The process was not always easy and often brought up difficult emotions. Despite the fear and shame that arose during the process, I approached the journey as if gazing into a mirror, facing a raw and unfiltered reflection of myself. Through it all, I've learned valuable lessons about myself and the world around me. I've gained a deeper understanding of and greater appreciation for the power of compassion and empathy. Overall, I've become a more resilient, wise, and compassionate person.

So, through tears, sometimes joyful ones, and often with a heavy heart, I wrote this book, knowing that the potential for a stronger, smarter, and kinder version of myself was on the other side.

DURING THE 2 A.M. HOUR

In the projects, somebody can call your mother
a one-legged whore who does nasty tricks for
men for five dollars, and she will still be the
most important and influential person in your
childhood. Even for children who grow to hate
their mothers, their hatred will be the most potent love they know.

No Disrespect, Sister Souljah

Shawn and I were the same age for three months each
year—a detail that mattered to us as kids. Shawn's mother
was one of my mom's younger sisters. My aunt babysat my
brothers and me throughout elementary school. Shawn
would do anything to get a giggle out of me. He was my best

friend for a minute. He struggled academically, and I had never heard of any attempts at remediation to help him. At about seven or eight years old, he still called sandwich "sammich" and potato chips "chayba chips." Much like the rest of us in Baltimore, he said dog as "dug," sink as "zink," and "muvva" instead of mother. As I got older, it became clear that Shawn's way of speaking wasn't just a quirky Baltimore thing. It was tied to his struggles in school, which went unnoticed and unattended.

When we were not playing "house," in which one of us was a parent and the other was a kid, we played "school." I was always the teacher standing over him with my bossiness and love of words. Frequently, I read to Shawn from the well-worn books my grandmother brought us home from her job as a custodian. Occasionally, I asked him to read to me. I scanned the pages with my pointer finger and consistently nudged him to sound out the words. Instead of teaching, I sometimes bellowed commands like, "Take that gum out of your mouth." "Sit down and be quiet." I enjoyed being the teacher because I was bossy, and words were magic.

No game could change the fact that the world was already letting him slip through the cracks.

§

In the 1970s, everyone on my mother's side of the family lived in the Cherry Hill projects. My grandmother and her six children shared a cramped three-bedroom row house on the 900 block of Bethune Road. Bethune Road buzzed with summer life: kids darting through broken fire hydrants, men polishing their car rims to perfection, and stereo speakers blasting music from screened windows.

When Aunt Peanut got approved for her own house in Cherry Hill, she moved into the 800 block of Bethune Road, just a one-minute walk to my grandmother's house. Years later, she and Shawn moved into the house just next door to my grandma. Meanwhile, my mom, my two brothers, and I lived three blocks away on Round Road. My older brother is 3 ½ years my senior, and our aunt Peanut babysat us while my mother worked as a bartender. When my mom got off work, she would call and tell my aunt to send us home. We walked the few treeless blocks in the dark. Sometimes we held hands.

§

In the 1980s and 1990s, my aunt paraded around in neon spandex bodysuits with shabby fringes and slits hand-cut into the sleeves. Her nails were dark and thick and curled like talons, often painted bright colors with glitter. She smoked, drank, and partied until addiction gripped her. Her words, sharp and fiery, often targeted Shawn and occasionally me.

Sometimes, she would look at me snidely and say, "You are too damn grown." Aside from Shawn, I received the lion's share of her beatings. Even though I did not endure them as often as her son, I still shudder at the sheer brutality. Beyond the screaming and name-calling, her favorite punishment was beating me on the back with her fist until my nose bled. Once, when I was about seven years old, she beat me on her front porch. She made me turn toward the street while screaming at me for playing in an abandoned car in the parking lot less than a block away.

"I told you not to play in that mothafuckin' car." Bam! With every syllable, she punched me. "YOU! TOO! GOD! DAMN! GROWN!" Bam! Bam! Bam! Blood poured from my nose to my chin and onto my shirt. I felt the warm wetness slide off my lips and drip onto the bright green grassy carpet that covered her half of the porch she shared with Ms. Mary as her other next-door neighbor.

She stormed through the aluminum screen door behind me, threatening to beat my fuckin' ass again if I took my grown self back to that abandoned car. Moments later, I went inside while tilting my head back as I walked upstairs. In the bathroom, I crammed toilet paper into my nose and mouth, muffling my sobs so she wouldn't hear. I sat on the toilet seat lid until she yelled for me to come downstairs and eat.

When I was close to 30 years old, my mom, my aunt Peanut, and I were in my mother's kitchen. Out of nowhere, my aunt said to me, "Do you remember when I used to hit you until your nose started bleeding? What would you do if I did that that now?"

"I would kick your ass." I don't use profanity in front of my mother, but I needed to say that.

"Sandra, did you hear what your daughter just said to me?" I was truly grown by then and had no qualms about telling her what I felt. I wished she would.

Speaking just above a whisper, my mother responded, "Uhn huh." My mother knew I was serious.

§

The beatings Shawn endured were worse. It happened whether the two of them were alone in the house or she was sharing her bed with some complicit boyfriend. My grandmother, just a wall away, often thumped on it and yelled for her to "Stop beating that boy like that!" Those must have been the absolute worst.

Her cruelty shattered something in Shawn. Telling him she wished she'd aborted him, combined with years of physical abuse, scarred him deeply and set him on a predictable path. By twelve, he was in and out of juvenile detention centers, then jails, then prisons.

When he was locked up, I occasionally wrote letters on my aunt's behalf because she struggled to write, just as Shawn did. She promised to send him money but rarely did. During the years before cell phones, the landline in her house was often disconnected, so when Shawn wanted to reach her from jail, he would have to call collect at my grandmother's house or Ms. Mary's. Someone would yell out the window for my aunt or knock on her door to let her know Shawn was on the phone. Though Aunt Peanut repeatedly promised to send him money, she followed through only a few times—$25 one time, $40 another.

§

My cousin earned the nickname 'Knuckles' for the bare-knuckle fighting skills he honed in prison. Like many incarcerated men, he exercised excessively and bulked up. Every time he came home, his mother couldn't resist squeezing his muscles, marveling at how strong he'd become.

Nothing was more consistent than Shawn's promises to our grandmother from jails and prisons. He meant it with every fiber of his soul each time he called her and said he was studying hard for his GED. As God was his witness, he would straighten up and fly right. He would be at her beck and call the second he got out, and she would never want for anything.

Grandma would take the bus downtown to visit him at the Baltimore City Jail, always ready to send money whenever he asked, no matter how many times he was locked up. He learned how to draw portraits and created sketches of her that she prominently displayed in her house. She bragged that Shawn was always doing well, taking up a trade, staying clean, and would be home any minute. Shawn ran up her phone bill with endless collect calls, but she always managed to scrape together enough to pay it.

On two occasions while I was on the East Coast, I drove my grandmother from Baltimore to a federal penitentiary in Pennsylvania to visit him. The first time was an absolute disaster. At the security checkpoint, an officer swiped my grandmother's hands and detected cocaine residue. She was devastated and sobbing because she did not know where it came from. She was equally upset about the possibility of not seeing him. Recognizing her age—she was in her seventies—and the likelihood that the residue came from handling dollar bills, they allowed her a brief 30-minute visit with Shawn. I remained in the car while they caught up during their quick visit. She was still profoundly annoyed about the residue mishap when she returned to the car and had not even hinted at a smile in the photo they took together that day.

My baby brother and Rose rode along during the second trip to Pennsylvania. Rose was Shawn's wife. I do not recall whether they met while he was in prison or during one of his short stints on the street. When Shawn left prison soon after our trip to Pennsylvania, he and Rose were doing well. He had only been out for a week when I visited them at her house in Baltimore. I videotaped Rose's teen kids and Shawn dancing to house music in their living room. For a little while, everything seemed terrific. That same videotape shows him gently helping our nearly 80-year-old grandmother in and out of my car in the snow, his tenderness unmistakable. He handled her gingerly as she got in and out of my car in the snow.

Barely a month after his 2005 release, I bought Shawn a plane ticket to visit me in California. He had never been on a plane before and was thrilled to escape the city for a few days. Getting permission from his parole officer required me to write a letter detailing our relationship, my role as a university professor, and our planned activities.

Being with Shawn transported me back to our childhood. I took him around the suburban California town where I live—a place that felt to him, as it still does to me, like a world away from home. I have a photo of him standing under an orange tree. He'd never seen oranges growing on the sidewalk. He enjoyed the slower lifestyle and told me he could see himself living here. He wondered if I could help him find work.

After being in California for four days and having just two nights before he was to return to Baltimore, I took him to a nightclub. While he and Rose stayed legally married, they were not together anymore. He met a woman at the club, and the two made plans to spend the night together. He borrowed my car to meet the woman two hours away at 2 o'clock in the morning. When he had not returned by dawn nor responded to my calls and texts, I reluctantly called the police and inquired about the possibility that he might have had an accident—or an incident.

I couldn't sleep, consumed by all the ways things could go wrong for a formerly incarcerated Black parolee in an unfamiliar state, driving an unregistered sports car to meet a stranger. The 911 operator said there had been no reports of accidents, and she became a bit huffy about it on my third call.

Right before 11 a.m., he came moseying through my front door, alive and smiling. He'd had a wonderful time.

Thank you, Lawd.

When I drove my cousin to the airport for his trip back

to Baltimore, I prayed he would feel inspired to get a job and stay out of trouble. Alas, Baltimore swallowed him whole again. Getting high with his mother exacerbated his problems. They deceived each other about how much cash and dope they had to share, and he frequently reminded her of his wretched childhood—to guilt her out of her last $5. His criminal behavior primarily consisted of robbing drug dealers.

§

Shawn was blessed with two sons, the oldest of whom carried his full name. My aunt spent time with the boys when they were young. She lavished them with affection and attention that she had never shown Shawn, my two brothers, or me.

At 17 years old, Shawn Jr. was shot in the head during the 2 a.m. hour, gunned down by multiple shooters for his gang activity. Shawn Jr. was the seventh teenager murdered in Baltimore in March 2007. Every one of them was African American. He was flown by helicopter to the University of Maryland Hospital, where he died in the shock trauma unit almost two hours later. As irony would soon reign, Shawn Sr. had the name of his son's gang tattooed on his back as a tribute.

The day her grandson was murdered, Aunt Peanut was brutally beaten by a man whose drugs she'd tried to steal. A helicopter airlifted her to the same shock trauma unit where her grandson had died just hours earlier. Her attacker faced an attempted murder charge, but it was dropped when her fear kept her from testifying. Months after the attack on his mother, Shawn orchestrated a confrontation with her assailant while locked up at the City Jail. With a hint of pride, my grandmother said, "Shawn beat that man within an inch of his life."

Consumed by grief and despair as he struggled to come to terms with the loss of his son, Shawn Sr. fell deeper into the abyss of depression and addiction. Despite everyone's pleas, he did not change. He admitted to me that he kept getting high to numb the pain he couldn't bear to feel. I tried to appeal to him from 3000 miles away but to no avail.

Shawn and his last girlfriend, Keena, had a volatile relationship marked by frequent fights, mutual violence, and relentless arguments. Neither of them worked. She accused him of stealing money from her to get high. Keena loved Shawn, and she was loyal to him. I once tried to mediate an argument between them when I witnessed him say to her, "Don't forget. I don't have a problem hitting females."

In 2007, Shawn and Keena were living with my mother when he and a friend allegedly killed two young men during a scuffle over a drug stash and cash. That night, my mother overheard Shawn confessing to Keena that the robbery wasn't meant to end in bloodshed. A poorly sketched illustration posted in the community and a reward for his capture led police cars and a helicopter to my mother's front door.

During the six months he spent in jail awaiting trial on first-degree murder charges, Shawn racked up drug debts he couldn't repay. Desperate for cash, he repeatedly called me with a flimsy story about needing $25 for shower shoes. The day after Shawn called me from jail for the last time, another inmate stabbed him and punctured one of his lungs. He was immediately admitted to the hospital.

When police arrested Keena on an unrelated warrant that could have led to a 25-year sentence, they offered her freedom in exchange for testifying against Shawn. She said she did not know anything about the murders. I wrote to her during the months she was jailed, reminding her of the years she would be in prison if she were found guilty. I reminded her that no man was worth sacrificing her life for. After hearing about my advice to Keena, Aunt Peanut confronted me brazenly with a swag she would not have been able to back up if things had gone south. She demanded to know if I'd told Keena to rat out her baby boy.

"Hell yeah, and you should go to the cops, too, if you know that he killed those guys." Aunt Peanut may or may not have known the details, but it was my mother whom the police picked up and interrogated for hours and hours. After lying in the hospital for two weeks, my cousin eventually exited jail with all charges dropped; the police could not gather enough evidence or witnesses to convict him.

By 2008, numerous paid hits had been on my cousin's life. Hence, few were surprised when shots rang out in Cherry Hill during the 2 a.m. hour one August morning. A year and five months after his son's death, Shawn Sr. was gunned down with five bullets to the back, becoming Baltimore's 118th murder victim of the year. My aunt and grandmother were shattered. We all were.

§

Shawn might have been a productive member of society if the neighbor who impregnated my aunt had given Shawn the love, resources, and truth he deserved. My cousin discovered in his late teen years that his father was the man who had lived on the other side of Ms. Mary, just two doors down from the house where Aunt Peanut and Shawn lived. The revelation that this married man with three kids was Shawn's father was appalling. My heart ached as I realized how his father's silence contributed to a cycle of violence and death that was preventable. In the face of our family's financial struggles, Shawn's father stepped forward and paid the funeral costs without comment. He is named in Shawn's obituary as the father of his beloved son.

The last time I saw my aunt was in March 2023, when my mother dialed me in for a video chat. Aunt Peanut was in a nursing home with advanced stages of cancer. She said, "I love you." I told her I loved her, too. I could hear her shallow, labored breaths.

She died two days later.

§

The cover photo of Shawn's obituary was taken in prison, like many of the other images in the montage inside. One image shows him in a cap and gown, marking the day he earned his GED behind bars. Another shows him in the visiting room, surrounded by his prepubescent sons, his mom, and my baby brother. My favorite among the obituary photos is the one that captures Shawn's essence—before life wore him down. It depicts Shawn as a kindergartener in a classroom, seated in a wooden chair that perfectly hugs his tiny body. That innocent moment frozen in time shows his smile radiating unblemished joy, devoid of the pain and hardships he would later face. It's a snapshot of limitless possibilities, of a potential that life would tragically cut short.

One obituary photo shows Shawn and Rose on their wedding day. Apart from Easter, when we were 4, 5, and 6, his wedding was the only time I saw him in a suit and tie. One more shows him with his arm draped around the neighbor's son—his brother—both nearly the same age.

I sometimes find solace in old videotapes, like the one where Shawn and Rose's children compete in a lively dance-off. Their joy and laughter leap from the screen. Later in the video, Shawn tenderly guides our grandmother across an icy path to my car—a fleeting moment of grace and care. These cherished moments reveal glimpses of the Shawn who existed beyond his troubles. They stand in stark, painful contrast to the harsh realities he endured, the battles he fought, and the demons that eventually consumed him.

To me, he'll always be the boy who said, "sammich" and believed every promise he made to our grandmother. A boy who deserved so much more. A man broken by the twin tragedies of losing his child and his childhood.

GOODBYE TO YESTERDAY

If you want total security, go to prison. There you're fed, clothed, given medical care, and so on. The only thing lacking is freedom.

Dwight Eisenhower

The first time I walked into a prison, just weeks before my 23rd birthday in 1992, I wore a stiff navy-blue polyester uniform with a clip-on bowtie, polished black combat boots a half size too big, and a royal-blue pin I'd earned at the academy. It poked through the inside of my shirt pocket like a badge of honor, though I soon learned it marked me as a rookie.

Prisons had fascinated me since middle school, thanks to my obsession with the Australian soap opera *Prisoner: Cell*

Block H. I imagined myself as a fly on the wall, absorbing the drama and human complexity within those walls. Unlike the women on that show, though, I hoped to avoid backstabbing, shoving matches, and revenge plots against the warden. I pictured myself standing in the middle of the chaos, blowing a whistle, and telling everyone to breathe.

Uncle Earl, a seasoned correctional officer, had worked everywhere—boot camps, women's prisons, supermax facilities, even Baltimore's city jail. During my visits to his house, I peppered him with questions. What did the inmates eat? Did they act like the people in movies? Had he met anyone notorious? His answers always left me hungry for more.

§

With a degree in psychology in hand, I applied to be both a probation officer and a correctional officer. Although I scored higher on the probation test, I couldn't resist the pull of working inside a prison. I requested a placement in a women's minimum-security facility, hoping for something manageable. A year of tests, background checks, and interviews later, I was offered a position—not at a women's prison, but at Maryland's newest maximum-security men's prison. My stomach flipped. Terrified, I said yes.

In July 1992, the Maryland House of Corrections Annex was a sprawling complex of six buildings, each capable of holding up to 384 prisoners. From the sky, each building looks like an X with perfectly spaced wings in which there are alphabetic designations (A, B, C, and D) for the buildings and the wings. At the time, only two buildings—'A' and 'B'— were finished. "A" building was the only one with three wings (A, B, and C wings), and it was the location for prisoners on segregation, with most already sanctioned for violations they committed in "B" building. Others awaited a hearing after being caught fighting, making alcohol, or some other egregious act.

"B" building housed protective custody (P.C.) inmates on one wing and the general population in the other three wings. Each wing of the buildings had an upper and lower tier, and every cell except for the lockup and protective custody wings contained two prisoners per cell. The four wings had an industrial washer and dryer on both levels, one dayroom with a TV and telephones, and an exit to their own yard. Hence, the 96 prisoners in B building, B wing did not ever interact with those on A, C, or D wings. However, some prisoners would stand behind the officer's desk at the glass opening of their wing and communicate using hand signals with others in the adjacent wing.

'B' building bustled with a fast-paced cacophony of metal doors opening and clanging shut, nonstop jeering about sports or board games, and a diverse range of men's loud voices. Depending on the area, there was abundant movement, energy, and urgency. Sunday afternoons at 1 o'clock were among the rare moments of calm, when prisoners sat captivated by *Soul Train*.

The prison shattered my expectations. It was louder, angrier. The control center, a glass bubble filled with equipment and no guns, held the tools of our trade: handcuffs, pepper spray, and radios. At the academy, they drilled into us that our only real weapons were our minds and mouths. Yet nothing could have prepared me for the stark reality of those wings.

§

My uncle was a highly regarded captain at the Annex. He maintained clear boundaries between prisoners and officers. Since he worked the 7 a.m. to 3 p.m. shift and I was part of the team that began at 3, I occasionally caught glimpses of him as he was leaving. I never publicly declared our relationship. He kept clear boundaries with inmates and officers alike. I respected him too much to let anyone know we were related. My father, a C.O. at the Baltimore City Jail, was also proud of my new career. At my graduation from the academy, he stood tall in his matching uniform.

Out of my class of 85, only five of us graduated with distinction. That's why I'd received the blue pin. Respect, I learned, wasn't given with the uniform. It had to be earned, often under pressure, and sometimes at a personal cost. I soon learned I could not rely on my badge to gain it. Although the paramilitary correctional officer academy provided me with essential knowledge, I learned quickly that on-the-job training was the only way to truly master the role of a C.O.

Most of the prisoners were Black men, as were many of the officers. Prisoners sometimes called us traitors and "house niggers," likening us to overseers on a plantation. They asked pointed questions, like, "Would you shoot me if I tried to get free?" It wasn't an escape to them. It was freedom. I deflected with policy-speak, but their questions haunted me. If someone did run, and if I were stationed in the tower, could I really pull the trigger? I never wanted to find out.

Weapons training drilled into us: if a prisoner escaped, we had to shoot to kill. They warned us that if an inmate escaped while we were stationed in a tower with a gun, we would be charged as co-conspirators and held accountable for any crimes they committed on the run. Fortunately, I was never assigned to the tower with a gun—it would have terrified me. It was overwhelming to think of firing a gun at someone, killing or missing them entirely, and then facing potential criminal charges. While I never explicitly said yes when men asked if I would kill them, I also avoided saying no. My responses typically revolved around reminding them that an escape violates the law.

§

Approximately three months into my new job, I saw an inmate worker collecting trash from the prisoners in solitary confinement. The man in the cell pushed out a large bag through the feeding slot and handed it to the worker, who placed it in a large industrial garbage can that he rolled from cell door to cell door. I approached the worker to inquire about the bag, assuming it was alcohol. It contained a light blue Fila-brand velour sweat suit. Prisoners were permitted to wear street clothes. I told them passing bags, clothes, or anything else was against the rules. They said the outfit belonged to the worker and was merely being returned.

I did not follow up, unfortunately. The next morning, I got a call from a supervisor informing me that the prisoner in the cell had accused me of allowing someone to steal his sweat suit. He had filed a grievance to demand I pay for a new one. He denied handing it off to a worker. I owed him a sweat suit since the violation occurred on my watch. They played me.

§

The officer's desk was at the entrance of the wing, just steps from the shower. I was too inexperienced to notice when men were masturbating while staring from the shower. I learned soon enough, though, and I began walking away from the desk, or I ignored the ones who repeatedly called me with bogus requests to help make sense of their legal documents.

One prisoner purposely and consistently extended his time in solitary confinement with minor infractions like flooding his cell because he feared returning to the general population. He was nicknamed 'Homicide.' A man of about twenty-five who was thin and dark-skinned, he had an awful reputation for masturbating as female officers walked the tier for security checks. He was not to be trusted.

During a midnight shift when I was drafted to stay, I worked the segregation unit where he was housed, "Homicide" kept trying to get my attention.

"Hey, C.O.!" He bellowed through the slit on the side of his door.

"What do you want, Mr. Johnson?" I lifted my head toward the upper tier, but I did not budge from my seat at the desk on the lower tier.

Amid the quiet, he yelled again. "Come here for a minute, C.O. I wanna ask you something."

"I can hear you from here, Mr. Johnson. What do you want?" I noticed other prisoners peering through the windows of their cell doors. They knew why he kept calling for me.

After I refused to go upstairs, he yelled, "Fuck you then! Ugly ass dyke." That earned him a write-up.

When I made my rounds, I walked upstairs and looked through each window to ensure a living body in every cell. Just inches after strolling away from Homicide's cell, he used the slit in the door to squirt liquid from a bottle at me. Squoosh! Prisoners in solitary often filled bottles with vile substances—urine, semen, or sour milk—as retaliation, disrespect, or a symptom of mental illness. I suspected 'Homicide,' who I later learned was incarcerated for rape, did it for all three reasons. As I walked to the edge of the tier and down the steps, showing no reaction, I heard him behind me, laughing loudly. A couple of others joined in.

"Damn, C.O. He shit you down. Ah ha!"

I felt the liquid on my skin and did not look back. Seconds after sitting at the desk, I looked at my arm and sniffed my shirt. The liquid was water. 'Homicide' chose to embarrass me rather than disgust me.

§

My biggest frustration came from working with some officers. Many were miserable humans who hated being there as much as the prisoners did. They were petty and mean-spirited, and it was difficult to feel a sense of solidarity with them.

I made the awful choice to go on a few dates with a coworker, a sergeant, who I knew was married. He told me he and his wife were on the outs, and since I wanted nothing more than to "spend time," I invited him over to my place. One night, his wife called to ask if I had been with her husband. Shocked and embarrassed, I conceded. Apparently, she confronted him after she hung up with me because he called within minutes, growling. "I'm going to fuck you up," was all he said before hanging up.

So, not only was the prison an uncomfortable place due to the constant risk of harm from inmates, but the job was also unsafe because a sergeant was going to 'fuck me up.' The sergeant was friends with my uncle, who had advanced to the rank of major by then. I was scared. Reluctantly, I phoned him and shamefully explained what had happened. He said he would take care of it. I never knew what he said, but the sergeant never talked to me again. I did, however, begin getting stationed on some of the more challenging wings to run.

§

The entire Maryland Division of Corrections required officers to work seven days at a time, with three days off, and then another seven days on with four days off. This rotation ensures fairness by providing the entire staff with at least one weekend out per month and certain major holidays. If the oncoming shift needed more officers to run the facility, those already working had the option to volunteer for overtime or would be drafted, meaning they would have no choice but to stay. On good days, I would sometimes choose to stay over for the extra cash, but if I'd had a bad day, I would be upset that I was forced to work another eight hours, which meant working through the night and not being allowed to sit for too long, read, or do anything else except make sure no one escaped.

Day in and day out, the job gnawed at me. I made a lot of money in those first 12 months. Having a gig making $40,000 as a single 23-year-old in the early 1990s might have been enough to keep others happy, but I was miserable. I was unsafe and exhausted.

When prisoners asked why I'd chosen this job, I'd say, 'I'm here to make a living,' though the answer never felt right. I knew my decision to work in prison had political implications for the Black men locked up there—and for me as a Black woman. But I never wanted to do the work of figuring out exactly what those implications were as long as I stayed there.

Like every other psychology major I'd met, I wanted to do good. I had always wanted to help people in whichever career I chose, and I never felt like my job as C.O. allowed me to fulfill that aspiration. Maryland taxpayers paid me to uphold a system that stifled, rather than nurtured, human potential.

Prisoners were locked in a system that did little more than warehouse them, and I was part of "the system." I felt for those who had turned their lives around or were so young as to have been tried as adults at 16 or 17. Many had been dealt a rough hand, with abusive parents or growing up in crack-infested neighborhoods.

Most of the men were starved for attention from women. A few of them told me to let them know if anyone gave me trouble so they could have my back. The men with whom I shared the most similarities were members of various Muslim groups. Their discussions about Black liberation inspired me. Muslims at the prison often espoused nationalist politics and preached about justice. Muslim brothers did not ask me trite questions about my bra size. They never expressed an interest in the rumors about me being a lesbian. During the month of Ramadan, I requested to supervise their nightly sessions, even though it meant sitting outside a dayroom on a wing in the otherwise empty 'C' building and not being able to hear their conversations.

Eddie was someone I liked. He lived in 'B' building on 'B' wing. Eddie was two years younger than I was and had been incarcerated since he was seventeen for being part of a group of young men who fatally assaulted another young man. As a Nation of Islam leader, Eddie always wore a bow tie and suit. Knowing my thirst for knowledge, he frequently quizzed me on vocabulary words. The only word he ever stumped me with was 'nefarious.' Even now, when I hear it, I think of Eddie tossing it to me through the feeding slot.

My uniform and everything it symbolized abandoned the possibilities of rich relationships between them and me. I wanted something different. I departed from the Maryland

Division of Corrections after 18 months because I couldn't stand having my safety on the line for eight or sixteen hours every day. The experience was a taxing and eye-opening journey that gave me a profound outsider-within experience I have carried throughout my life.

I had not shared with anyone the date I was leaving. Eddie knew I would come to his cell and say goodbye when the date arrived. For months, he questioned if that would be the day. I worked the 7 a.m.–3 p.m. shift on my last day. Once the count cleared and I was about to depart, I walked over to the building and wing where Eddie stayed, looked in the window of his cell, and motioned for him to come to the door.

"This is it. I'm done," I uttered, my voice trembling with excitement and sadness.

"Aww, wow. For real?"

I nodded, a lump forming in my throat. "Yeah. I'll stay in touch, though. You take care of yourself, hear?" I tried to sound firm. I felt heavy.

As I exited the building and turned the corner towards the first gate, a powerful song blasted through the crack of Eddie's open window. *It's So Hard to Say Goodbye to Yesterday* by Boyz II Men filled the air, its soulful melody swirling around the compound. I was shaken. Tears streamed down my face as I stopped and leaned against the fence. I leaned against the fence for more than a minute. "It's so haaard. To say goodbye. To yesterday." I felt no shame or regret. It was a moment of unabashed vulnerability. I could detect Eddie's silhouette through the window.

Years later, I reconnected with Eddie after he was transferred to a minimum-security prison. I visited him, and we laughed about the day of my departure and how dramatic it had been.

Now, I watch his life unfold on social media—a life of family, travel, and triumph. He's no longer the boy in the bow tie, quizzing me through a feeding slot. He's a man, living the life he always deserved. I've seen his children grow up, his marriage flourish, the installation of an inviting in-ground pool in the backyard of his beautiful home, the opening of his own restaurant, and the numerous countries he and his family have joyfully explored.

§

I lasted 18 months at the Annex. By the end, I was exhausted. The job was a relentless grind, gnawing at my sense of safety and self. I had come to help people, but I felt like a cog in a machine that did little more than warehouse human beings. The prisoners weren't the only ones trapped. I was too.

Leaving the Annex was more than quitting a job. It was the start of a journey to redefine my relationship with the prison system and the people within it. I wanted more than a paycheck. I wanted connection, passion, and purpose. No more badges or blue pins. Just my open heart and a willingness to learn more about people. While the Annex provided me with crucial insights into the inner workings of prisons from a security perspective, it also served as a catalyst for realizing that merely hearing about prisoners' daily routines fell short of satisfying my deep longing to be integrated into their lives. I yearned to engage with them on a personal level, forge authentic friendships, extend kindness and support, and bear witness to their transformative journeys. This realization fueled my unwavering commitment to redefine my relationship with the entire prison system over the past 30 years.

My uncle and my dad found fulfillment in their work as

officers, and both stayed long enough to retire from the Division. I needed something different—something more. I wanted new connections, like the one I built with Eddie. I wanted a rewarding career that gave me time off to engage in volunteer work. I could no longer reconcile my internal struggle with being firm and impartial.

Through this journey, my curiosities have soared, affirming my enduring desire to connect with incarcerated people in a way that transcends the boundaries of the uniform I once wore. No more relying on the symbols of authority; no more ribbons and badges. Instead, I wear my heart on my sleeve, and I am driven by a genuine desire to bring about positive change.

I don't know where this road is going to lead—.

THE LEGEND OF JOE EDISON
(TAKE TWO)

It's true that pain makes people change.

Kid Cudi

In my 2007 self-published memoir, *If My Soul Be Lost*, I wrote a chapter about Joe Edison, a brother from my 'hood who served a long sentence at the prison where I worked after college. In "The Legend of Joe Edison," I explained that he and I grew up during the 1970s and '80s in Cherry Hill, a large project community in south Baltimore, where we referred to him as "Joe Edison," never just "Joe."

My grandmother once described how he killed the wrong person but escaped jail and ultimately found his intended target. My aunt swore he boldly strutted around the neighborhood in women's clothes, evading the police. My cousin added that he made it onto *America's Most Wanted.*

In the summer of 1986, as I prepared to enter my senior year of high school, Joe Edison shot a young man in the face on a playground, suspecting him of snitching to the police. That playground sat between two elementary schools in Cherry Hill—one of which I had attended from kindergarten through third grade. Joe Edison was also charged with shooting at a cop. He walked out the front door of the Baltimore City Jail in February 1987 while awaiting trial for murder and attempted murder.

When I asked how he pulled it off, he said,

When I asked how he escaped, he said, "I packed my clothes, got a pass, and left. I went from the fourth to the first floor, through the tunnel, showed my pass, and walked out. They opened the door, took my fingerprint, lifted the gate, and I was on Madison Street." In September of 1987, the police finally caught him.

§

I first met Joe Edison in 1992, as a correctional officer on the 3–11 p.m. shift in 'B' Building on 'C' Wing. Known as one of the Annex's toughest wings, it housed 96 men, at least half of whom roamed the wing freely when I arrived. The chaos was overwhelming. I darted between tiers, ordering prisoners to return to their cells or the dayroom. One locked in, and another spilled out. The scene was whack-a-mole madness. They ignored me entirely. I desperately needed help.

Amid the chaos, one prisoner demanded that I make a call regarding his visit, the nurse, or a package—I cannot recall which one. He became increasingly irate when I did not move swiftly enough. He moved in closer to my face, and his body language suggested he was about to strike me. I took a step back, and he stepped forward. Despite his skinny build, he towered over me. As he got louder in his demand for whatever he asked for, the men of C Wing grew quieter. I glanced back at the officer in the control booth, and his facial expression suggested that I had better get things under control.

"Bald-headed bitch!" he screamed before turning on his heel.

"She ain't got no business being in here anyway," another yelled from a few feet away.

My panic was apparent, and I wanted to leave. I walked backward toward the entrance door of the wing and radioed for someone to relieve me. While I waited, I noticed about 30 people staring at me, including the piercing green eyes belonging to Joe Edison.

The man who wanted me to do something for him uttered more expletives as he walked up the steps to the second tier. I felt the heat of eyes boring into me. At that moment, I glanced up and locked onto a pair of piercing green eyes: Joe Edison's. He stood at a distance, calm and detached. I silently willed him—or anyone—to intervene, but he didn't. He didn't know me, and the blue polyester uniform marked me as something other than a homegirl from Cherry Hill. He observed silently, then went about his business.

News spread throughout the facility that I had lost control of C Wing. Prisoners and officers later gossiped about my inability to maintain control, and I was viewed as weak for asking for help. I never wanted to work the wing again, and I instantly began thinking how soon my next career move would happen. I soon took a leave of absence and returned only for a few months before leaving the prison for good.

§

In 2008, Eddie—the prisoner who'd once stumped me with the word "nefarious"—called from a minimum-security prison. "Hold on," Eddie said. "I got somebody here who wants to talk to you."

"Nandy?" The voice was raspy, almost playful. "It's Joe Edison."

"Oh, my goodness! Hey, Joe!" I stammered, both surprised and intrigued.

"I read your book," he said. His voice carried a hint of amusement.

"I hope it was okay." I tried to sound casual but felt nervous. I hadn't expected him to read it, let alone contact me.

He asked if I would write his biography, and I told him I would consider it. He asked if I'd write his biography. I told him I'd consider it, but only after we met in person. A few months later, I sat across from him at a round table in the visiting room of a minimum-security prison in Jessup, Maryland. When he walked in wearing a collared shirt and an argyle sweater vest, I couldn't reconcile his polished appearance with the tales of chaos and violence that had defined his reputation.

His furrowed brow and piercing gaze suggested he was heavily invested. He had spent most of his adult life scrutinizing the meaning of hand gestures, studying the direction and weightiness of footsteps, and listening to what people intended rather than what they said. In our two-hour conversation, he told me he pays close attention to his surroundings. If he detected a threat, he approached a person calmly—and stabbed them.

"Ain't no fights in prison. Just stabbings," Joe Edison casually remarked.

"Oh, okay. Well, how many people have you stabbed?" I was shocked at my confidence in asking.

"In the last 22 years since I've been here... 'bout 10, I think." Joe Edison said this immodestly while searching in his head to confirm the number.

"Have you been stabbed before?"

"I got nipped on my face one time." He beckoned the air near the faint scar on his left cheek. "That li'l mark is gone now."

Joe Edison shared an experience that reminded me of how cruel prisoners can be. A random prisoner mistakenly received a letter intended for him. Rather than pass it on, the man responded to the letter—written by Joe Edison's mom—by spreading feces on it before mailing it back to her.

The cops beat Joe Edison during one of his arrests in the '80s and knocked out a few of his front teeth. He offered only half-smiles as we sat across from each other, but I saw his veneers through a smirk while he talked about being on the witness stand during one of his life-sentence appeals.

"The judge told me I was the most articulate person he ever heard. I had people crying in that courtroom," he recalled.

"What did you say while you were on the stand?"

"I said I ain't do it. I told them I hated whoever did it, and if I could, I would breathe my own life into that man so that he could live, and I could die."

Joe Edison casually mentioned packing a knife to the visiting room to kill his daughter's mother. He did not follow through because his best friend grabbed him just before he exited the cell and said, "She ain't worth it."

I asked him if he was currently dating someone, and he piped up with a resounding yes.

"How did y'all meet?" I was being nosey.

He explained that the woman had seen him two years prior at a family-day event while visiting a relative. She inquired about Joe Edison, and the two became romantically entwined soon after meeting. They made plans to live together upon his release.

When was the last time you cried, Joe?" I asked. The silence was staggering. As I waited, I thought about the unsolved crimes we couldn't discuss, and the two life sentences he successfully appealed. I remembered the exaggerated stories of him wearing women's clothes to evade detection while on the run. The other visitors were noticeably rubbing pregnant bellies and stroking legs while Joe Edison and I searched for ways to muddle through a tough conversation about vulnerability. His right hand coddled his chin as his left hand nestled his right elbow. His lips were pinched and twitched upward. He was stuck, so I thought I would help.

"Did you cry when you read the book Redemption you told me about in a letter?"

"I cried, but ain't no tears fall. I think it was that day I was gon' stab my daughter's mother." I pretended to be unafraid.

I thanked him for allowing me to visit. We hugged and promised to stay in touch.

While driving back to my mother's house, I was pensive and still shocked by his candor.

§

I woke up one spring morning and noticed Joe Edison's ill-gotten prison cell phone number on my caller ID. I was alarmed by his urgent request to call him back as soon as possible. When I returned his call, he was sobbing uncontrollably.

"She's dead! My girl is dead!"

"What?" I was struck by the rawness in his voice and the fact that Joe Edison was crying.

"Slow down. Tell me what happened."

"Her ex broke into her house, shot her, then turned the gun on his'self."

Joe Edison described this relationship as his first intimate partnership in over twenty years. He admitted to opening himself up to her, loving her, and wanting to protect her. He was sure she loved him as well. If only he had known this would happen, he would have walked off the daytime job he was allowed to hold as a pre-release inmate and prevented it.

Joe Edison learned through the news that the murder-suicide wasn't committed by her ex-boyfriend. He was her live-in lover who discovered she was having an affair. Joe Edison was the *other* man. I listened, offered support, and checked on him over the next few days.

We spoke a couple of times upon his release. Once, he called while I was riding in the car with my mom. I put him on speakerphone and mouthed to her, "This is Joe Edison." Her jaw dropped in disbelief that I was speaking to *the* Joe Edison.

The last time I spoke to him, I wondered if he had found peace. His legend had loomed large over my childhood. In adulthood, I saw the man behind the myth—a human being wrestling with his own demons, searching for connection in a world that had long denied him one.

Even now, I think of him—not as the man from my

grandmother's stories or the prisoner who watched me cower, but as someone whose humanity I glimpsed for a fleeting moment.

FLOWERS GROW IN WINTER

Perhaps it's the decade between Halim's birth and mine, the contrast of our genders, or the 45 miles separating Baltimore and D.C., that explains our divergent paths—his to prison, mine to college. As a Black girl coming of age in inner-city Baltimore, my teenage years were full of the typical drama that led to fights, fleeting hookups, cruel gossip, and the arrogance of precocious kids from 'round the way. For Halim, "typical" in Washington, D.C., meant drugs, shootings, and survival—by any means necessary.

At 16, Halim Flowers was convicted as an accessory to the murder of a 52-year-old African American man. Tried as an adult, he was eleven years into a 30-to-life prison sentence when I wrote to him after seeing HBO's *Thug Life in D.C.* The documentary, focused on the juvenile block of the D.C.

Jail, gave a haunting glimpse into the lives of young Black boys awaiting trial for murder. Halim, guilty as charged, admitted that neither therapy nor juvenile detention could have turned him around back then. By 16, he had been arrested three times, twice for gun charges—including one for shooting at two teenagers—and once for accessory to murder. The day before his final arrest, he had just returned from juvenile detention.

I got a glimpse of the juvenile block of the D.C. Jail while watching HBO in the early 2000s. I often used the episode in my classes to demonstrate the connectedness of racial inequality, Black masculine expression, poverty, and crime. The youth featured in the film appear to be undereducated, low-income, and hyper-masculine. Every single one of them is Black. Most were awaiting murder trials.

In one unforgettable scene, the warden asked Halim how much time he was facing.

"They trying to give me 30 to life. I guess I can have kids when I'm 46. I might as well stay locked up for the rest of my life," he said, his boyish face impossibly younger than 16.

I wrote him a letter. It began an exchange of over 200 emails, countless phone calls, and one face-to-face visit. Halim became the kind of friend who could hold space for everything—our debates, shared discoveries, and the raw truths we offered each other.

§

He once told me Black women are fragile and beautiful. I saw how his Muslim faith inspired him to think of women differently from how I saw myself. Born into a family of Nation of Islam Muslims, Halim's layered perspectives on social justice issues deeply reflected the politics of race, men's and women's roles, and critiques of the criminal justice system. Sometimes, our conversations got heated, but we always circled back to our friendship with compassion and respect. Our divergent perspectives were often epistemological. Many of our chats focused on books we read, lessons I taught, his daily routine, his dreams of being a millionaire business owner, and prison. He mentored younger brothers and spent most of his days reading, meditating, exercising, and imagining his future as an artist. I often told him I wished my students shared his insatiable thirst for knowledge.

Considering how smart he was, as evidenced by what I saw of him at 16 and engaging him as he approached 30, I wondered why he made such poor choices as a child. He told me he sold drugs from ages 12 to 16 and "did all the normal things associated with that lifestyle, including having sex since age eleven," using marijuana and PCP, gambling, and committing violence. He added:

> I always went to school high on weed or boat (PCP). I stopped doing homework in the 7th grade. I used to have teachers cry tears to me because I would come to school and ace all their tests but never come to class except on test days. They said it made them and the other students look bad and that I was wasting talent. I wanted the streets, the jails, and the pain.

Throughout those years, his mother held a steady middle-class job during the day and pursued her college education at night. She moved him and his siblings to the suburbs when he was 13. She was always accessible, never caused them harm, and poured her emotional, financial, and spiritual resources into fulfilling her children's needs.

Therefore, I wanted to know why he was drawn away from the safety of her home and found the streets so alluring. Halim shared the following in an email:

> My mother could not really control me after my dad left. She put me out when I skipped court and violated my probation, but she eventually let me back in. She tried to beat me when I was younger. Then I got too big for that. She tried counseling. Everything. She even left me down south one summer when I was 13.
>
> I would tell her that the money from selling drugs came from shooting dice. When she found drugs, I told her I was only holding them for someone else. It was funny to me when I was in the D.C. Jail, and I told her that I was selling drugs; she was in shock. I could not believe how much she trusted all the lies I told her back then.
>
> I came in with shopping bags every week—hundreds of shoes and clothes. My friends had cars. I don't really know how to drive, but I would buy cars for other people to drive. I was too little to drive back then. I really hurt my mother. I even sold drugs to her sister, my aunt. I felt terrible when my aunt offered me sex for drugs. I knew then that I had to stop selling crack. I even looked for a job and started selling weed and PCP, and I couldn't find a job.
>
> One time, this girl was arguing with her

mother about selling all their food stamps for crack and having no food to eat. The girl came outside, and I was right there counting the food stamps and the first of the month's check money. She gave me a look that I could never forget.

Halim was transparent and always willing to share details of his life. So, I asked an abundance of questions, beginning with, "What the hell happened that landed you in prison?" He explained:

What happened was that I was drunk. Whenever I got drunk, I got liberal with my money. I lost a lot of money gambling, so I got even drunker and smoked more weed. A guy told me about a smoker [a PCP user] who had a lot of money in an apartment around the corner and gave me a gun. I'm moving without thinking, so I rush into the apartment. I just pulled out the gun on the guy, and he gave me a stack of money too big for my little hand to grab.

I'm not even aware of my surroundings when the two older guys grabbed me. I fired a shot into the wall, and we tussled for the gun—me against three grown, scared men. I don't know how the hell I got out of there alive with the gun. The gun jammed up on me, and that is why I didn't shoot them. Thank God for that. After I got out of there, my senses hit me, and my high was gone. I was mad at myself for being so stupid because I was never a good robber, just a good salesman.

I got around the corner and told two guys what happened. One of the guys got frustrated, took the gun from me, and walked back in that direction. The one who gave me the gun decided to pursue him back to the apartment. When we bent the corner, we heard three shots, and somebody yelled that such and such shot Butch.

For his role, Halim was sentenced to 30 years to life—a punishment that seemed draconian for a teenager. He told me he accepted the time but wrestled with what it revealed about America's justice system.

§

Ms. Martha, a 63-year-old Christian woman, contacted me shortly after Halim received my first letter. She had launched a campaign for his release, arguing that his sentence reflected systemic racism and a failure to account for his youth. She asked me to join her efforts by signing petitions and forwarding letters to celebrities and politicians. While I admired her dedication, I resisted. I wanted to know Halim for myself before joining the cause.

Ms. Martha's passion sometimes undermined her strategy. Her press releases often linked to a hip-hop magazine she ran that featured scantily clad women and flashy cars—imagery I feared would damage Halim's credibility. When I gently suggested removing the magazine's name, she balked. To her, the magazine was integral to his story.

My initial resistance was to the deluge of emails she sent me, tagged as urgent and requesting that I contact her immediately to let her know I had received and forwarded the letters. She redrafted letters to Obama and others she thought would give Halim's case significant media attention. I expressed that I was too busy to work on the campaign the way she wanted. In addition to his age, Ms. Martha consistently advanced issues that I needed time to unpack: Halim had paid his debt to society already; Halim was a wayward child who was now an extraordinary man; Halim was a victim of a racist criminal justice system; the Black community failed Halim. I was still grappling with the fact that Halim was guilty. Ms. Martha continued contacting me, asking if I had signed the petitions, read her press releases, and forwarded campaign letters. I asked her to give me time.

I asked if, in the meantime, I could suggest that the press releases not have her magazine title as the heading. If one followed the link to her magazine, one would have found a series of stories and images that I thought would diminish her efforts to reexamine Halim's case. For example, one section of the magazine is reminiscent of Jet Beauty centerfolds but with more of an "urban" flair. The "Fantasy" section was described as "visual eye candy. Lovely ladies, sexy as they wanna be. We only showcase the women that make you do a double take. We are always looking for lovely ladies passionate about modeling and getting attention." Why include the magazine name and link on the press releases?

In many of my conversations with Halim, he reiterated Ms. Martha's positions on racism, the system, surviving the 'hood, etc. I asked Halim to imagine an exclusive club of people with the key to open prison doors and allow inmates to go free, but they would only do so if they believed those people were contrite and safe to be around. I insisted that it was important not to give the impression that materialism and flashy cars aligned with his aspirations. People of influence want to know that Halim is redeemed.

I suggested reframing the narrative he and Ms. Martha constructed by demonstrating that he a) had gained a deep awareness of his childhood choices, b) was remorseful, and c) had a new outlook on life that would catapult him away from the trappings of "eye candy" and "whipz." I wanted him to be frank in his appeal that he chose to sell drugs, skip school, get high, and hang out with people who were going nowhere fast. And I longed for Halim—the poetic soul, the devout Muslim with the mark of unwavering devotion on his forehead, the adult who prefaced many of his statements with "As a man"—to conclude those very sentences with the admission: "I accept the responsibility for the harm, fear, and disrespect I inflicted upon others and the communities I harmed by my actions." While he acknowledged his role in the crime, I wanted him to stop repeating the point that he did what he "had to do to survive." I saw Halim and his tiny man-self on HBO when he struggled to hold up pants too big for him, but I knew him as a conscious 27-year-old who could open all kinds of opportunities for himself if he adopted a more mature version of his past and vision for his future.

Interestingly, Halim held a similar belief in holding me accountable. In an email to me, he wrote:

> I could see if I was an isolated menace. However, since my imprisonment, I have witnessed Columbine, Virginia Tech, gang numbers increasing, teenage pregnancies increasing, STD youth numbers increasing, juvenile incarceration increasing, college enrollment numbers for Black males decreasing, unemployment for Blacks increasing, diabetes, and

youth obesity increasing. You have failed.

As the exclusive learned club of this society whose responsibility is to formulate the ideas that will influence the politicians who legislate the laws to protect this nation and to guide the judicial branch that dispenses justice to our citizens, as the activists and social educators, you have failed.

Too many secret meetings and not enough public results. You have the doctorates and the debt to show for your sociological indoctrination but no social improvements in your communities. Our mothers, aunts, fathers, brothers, sisters, uncles, and neighborhoods are still cracked out, drug-infested, heavily diseased, miseducated, and suffering from poverty and economic under-development. Our schools are still failing big time.

If you never find that I express remorse, I've been judged already. What about the next generation? What will your exclusive social club do to save them from my fate? If the senseless youth violence continues, I won't be to blame. I'm here. I'm the menace, the one to be locked away for 30 years.

It's the social educators, scholars, and activists that will be blamed for not being creative enough to transfer their textbook savvy and secret meeting jargon into the real world of frustrated, scared, and hurting youth to create a healthy environment for children to not join gangs, carry weapons, use drugs, get pregnant, get abortions, and kill each other.

Damn. In just one email, Halim deservedly served me my ass on a platter. I had been pushing him to take responsibility for social issues greater than himself, and he unequivocally broke some shit down to be about my responsibility as a scholar who talks the talk but doesn't walk far enough for our words to matter. Most of us don't roll up our sleeves and dirty our hands on behalf of the young brothers I saw in the documentary.

He wasn't wrong. His words forced me to confront my own shortcomings as a scholar and activist. Halim's words struck a chord deep within me, stirring the long-standing guilt that has plagued me for over two decades of teaching at a suburban university with limited opportunities to engage with individuals from our communities. I have not lived in a city or worked directly in predominantly Black communities for nearly 25 years. While my primary approach to giving back has been to support incarcerated people through mentoring, professional endeavors, and friendships, I feel I should be doing much more.

§

After a year of not connecting with Halim, I sent him a handful of books from Amazon as well as Pierre Bourdieu's pivotal work on cultural capital, which profoundly impacted his thinking. Bourdieu examines how cultural knowledge and skills shape social inequality, arguing that individuals possess multiple types of capital—economic, social, and cultural—which help maintain social hierarchies. He identifies three forms of cultural capital—embodied (habits and knowledge), objectified (material items), and institutionalized (credentials)—and argues that privileged groups gain greater access to these resources, making cultural capital a powerful driver of hidden inequality. He asserts that cultural capital is unequally distributed, with privileged people having greater access to prestigious cultural practices and resources, meaning cultural capital operates as a hidden source of societal inequality. Halim loved thinking about equity in these ways, so we talked extensively about Bourdieu.

He called one day while I was driving to let me know he had received the items in the mail. I was pleased to hear his voice and pulled off the highway to talk to him. He said he'd had time to reflect on our conversations and had matured a lot. I expressed having done the same. His tone contained Buddhist underpinnings and conveyed selflessness, personal accountability, and a tinge of humility I had not heard from him before. He also wrote his autobiography, titled Contrition of a Man, after spending months marinating on how I had challenged him to think critically about remorse. I told him his words affected me, too. He reminded me that redemption is possible for all of us—even me.

Soon after that conversation, I dedicated considerable time and abundant resources to fly from California to the prison where he was housed in New Jersey. Unfortunately, several setbacks limited our visit: traffic congestion, retrieving my lost cell phone from a gas station, a two-hour wait for the prison's population count, and a strict deadline for my return to the airport. Halim and I had less than an hour together. In that brief visit, I recognized his genuine spirit. We promised to remain friends after his release and snapped a single cherished photo—the only in-person meeting we've had in our 15-year friendship.

§

Halim emerged as a rising star after 22 years of incarceration. People are enamored with him. In a recent phone chat, he and I agreed that his ambition is new only to people who have just met him. He has done remarkable things with his life in the free world. He has engaged in artist residencies across multiple countries, delivered a captivating TEDx Talk, and continues to be sought after as a speaker. The last time I spoke to him in May 2023, he said he had just arrived in France.

"What are you doing in France?" I was impressed.

"I'm over here for an art show. I'll be heading to London tomorrow."

"Wow. That's amazing. Have you been to London before?" I asked.

"Yeah, I go to London all the time. It's one of my favorite places." The pitch of his voice made it seem like London was around the corner, and of course, he goes there all the time. Doesn't everybody? Upon returning to the States, he sent me a video link to a French news report of his art show.

From the moment I met him in his 20s until now that he is in his 40s, he has consistently demonstrated the mission quoted on his website: to love everyone unconditionally all the time. Our friendship has been fortified by years of respectful debate, kindness, and growth inspired by each other. We remain friends because he allows himself to be vulnerable and trusts me enough to stand in his truth. He has always asked little of me, mostly that I stay true to the principles that he and I learned while growing up in the Black inner city, which taught us to reach back and snatch others from the embers of self-destruction, lest nothing be left for us to go home to except death, rage, and despair.

OG J

Do everything you can to make it around the
system, over the system, or out the system.

Tupac Shakur

When J speaks to my students about his days as a bank
robber, a bittersweet nostalgia washes over him. His grin
widens, his eyes brighten, and he animates the thrill of his
heists like a cinematic storyteller. He recounts the
adrenaline of each job and the rush of getting away clean.
But J's reflections don't stop at the thrill. He acknowledges
the ripple effects of his choices—the harm he caused his
children, wife, parents, and community. J now sees how the
leadership skills he once employed to execute crimes could
have been harnessed for building up the people he loves.

That revelation, heavy and humbling, reveals how far he has come. But it wasn't always this way. Back then, our debates were fiery and frequent.

§

I met J in the early 2000s during one of my workshops at the United States Penitentiary in Atlanta. I'd been invited to lead a discussion on the intersections of hip-hop culture and sexism, a topic guaranteed to spark heated exchanges. The room was full of incarcerated Black men, each with a unique perspective. J sat silently, but his presence was impossible to ignore. His poised demeanor and the intensity in his eyes told me he had plenty to say—he just wasn't ready to share it.

Later, J contacted me at the university to ask if he could enroll in one of my correspondence courses. His submissions were diligent and exhaustive, but what struck me most was their depth. His writing was alive with questions about social justice, racism, and the structural oppression of Black people. A devoted Rastafarian, J's worldview was rooted in Black liberation. He wore red, black, and green beads around his neck, and every inch of his existence seemed to vibrate with a love for our people.

But our conversations weren't easy. I challenged him to see the intersections between race and gender, to acknowledge that the fight for racial equality is incomplete without a reckoning with sexism. I asked J to think critically about the ways toxic masculinity, even within hip-hop culture, perpetuates harm. It wasn't just about naming the forces that oppressed him. I asked him—and the roomful of Black men listening—to confront their agency, their complicity in harm, and the power they held to create change.

J didn't always agree with me, especially about gender politics. His vision of Black liberation was often tangled in strict definitions of love and family. To him, Black love wasn't just personal; it was a political act. For years, he resented Black men who sought companionship with White women, seeing their choices as betrayals of Black solidarity. He even struggled to reconcile his beliefs with the interracial marriages of his daughter and sister. For J, the fight for racial equality wasn't just systemic; it was intimate, entwined with the love Black men and women poured into each other. Over time, he began to loosen his grip on those convictions.

§

Like many incarcerated people I know, J felt justified in the actions of his youth. He was doing time for bank robbery, which he felt was a political act to disrupt the White-dominated power structures and return them to the marginalized and oppressed. His political perspectives were straightforward and nuanced, intricately tied to his experiences, and he showed a lack of remorse for the damage he caused to the White establishment.

The distinction between political and politicized prisoners is essential. Political prisoners, in the strictest sense of the word, are rare in America. Political prisoners are jailed for their beliefs, anti-establishment, religious, or even anarchist beliefs. Unlike many other countries, the United States generally does not imprison individuals for what they believe. Based on political views, someone may commit criminal acts motivated by their disdain for the established order of the government. For instance, someone who kidnaps a head of state out of a belief that the latter's actions are oppressive towards the folks they were elected to serve could be considered to have committed a political criminal act.

Political prisoners often perceive the victims of their crimes as casualties in the liberation struggle. J's closest comrade in prison, Dr. Mutulu Shakur ("Doc"), was a former member of the Black Liberation Army and the stepfather of the late rapper Tupac Shakur. Convicted of multiple crimes, including armed bank robbery, murder, and conspiracy to aid Assata Shakur's escape, a fellow Black Liberation Army member, Doc, received a 60-year sentence. However, in 2022, he was granted a compassionate release due to his battle with stage four cancer after serving 37 years. Doc joined the ancestors on July 6, 2023.

Similarly, Indigenous activist Leonard Peltier has been in prison since 1977. He became a target of the FBI's counterintelligence program (COINTELPRO) due to his advocacy for promoting Indigenous sovereignty and rights. Peltier maintains his innocence to this day.

Mumia Abu-Jamal, an African American journalist and former Black Panther, is another well-known political prisoner who was sentenced to death in 1982 for the alleged murder of a police officer. His sentence was commuted to life without the possibility of parole.

Mumia, Doc, and Peltier represent prominent examples of individuals targeted by the government for their political ideas and involvement in race-based social movements that dared to speak truth to power.

According to J, robbing banks was a political act aimed at disrupting capitalism, as banks are the foundation of the government's economic structure. However, it is essential to note that J himself was not a political prisoner. He became politicized.

J studied political theory and social justice issues during

his incarceration. This process transformed him into a politically conscious person who advocated for the marginalized. He challenged the unfair treatment he perceived from the American government. J believed that acts such as bank robbery, attacking police officers, and arson of government buildings were forms of resistance against the unfairness perpetrated by the White elite and individuals in positions of power. He saw these actions as a way to bring attention to the systemic injustices he witnessed. Like other politicized prisoners, J dedicated himself to studying and spending time with people who shared his awakened consciousness.

J wasn't just a bank robber. In prison, he was a shot-caller. Alongside his closest comrade, Dr. Mutulu Shakur—stepfather to Tupac Shakur—J helped negotiate peace among factions and maintain order in the Atlanta penitentiary. They had rules: no snitching, no drugs, no tolerance for sex offenders. Under their leadership, violence decreased, and solidarity among incarcerated men increased. They were leaders within their confinement, even as they railed against the system that put them there.

In addition to his disdain for rapists and snitches, J's views on law enforcement were uncompromising. He considered correctional officers, police, and other "agents of the state" complicit in the oppression of Black people. In one of our many exchanges, he wrote:

"By the same token, I am not into giving a C.O. a pass just because he is living his life or doing it for his family. When you look at the entire system of justice and the laws that it creates—how America sucks the life out of whole countries and cultures, how capitalism and the prison industrial complex work to create a permanent subclass—

then you understand that each part of the system ties into the next. A correctional officer is as much a part of the system as a pilot dropping a bomb on Iraqi civilians, a politician lining his pockets, or a corrupt cop beating suspects and stealing their money and drugs. The whole system is fucked up, and everybody should be held accountable. Are the wealthy held liable? Are the polluters of the earth held responsible? Are Bush and Cheney held accountable for the mayhem, death, and destruction they caused? No. So why should I excuse a C.O. just because they're doing their job?"

He urged that the whole nation is a grotesque monster, gorging itself on the lives of the less fortunate while those in control profit. I agree that this isn't justice, not by any stretch of the imagination. It is exploitation disguised as law and order, oppression parading as freedom. And while I concede that it is a machine of destruction and we're all cogs in it, whether we're aware of it or not, I do not believe in the matter-of-fact distinctions he made between the haves and the have-nots.

I responded,

> "You place yourself at the heart of the system
> you despise. Yes, the system is unjust, but
> aren't you accountable for your role in it? You
> chose actions that landed you in prison. Blam-
> ing the system without addressing personal
> accountability won't bring liberation. I'm not
> saying this to put you down, Brotha, but if you
> want to keep it real, consider that the 13th
> Amendment of the Constitution justifies the
> slavery of people who commit crimes. You
> chose to become a part of the slave system, but
> you're mad at the people whose job keeps you

on the plantation.

As much as J railed against America, he placed himself smack in the middle of its criminal justice system. Yes, it's unjust, broken, and feeds on the suffering of disadvantaged people. But the bank robberies he committed were not politically motivated at the time he committed them, and the outcome of those crimes did nothing to tip the scales of power in our favor. We live in an unjust society with corrupt individuals; there is no denying that. But isn't personal accountability a factor, too? We can't just lay the blame on "the system." Yes, fight the power, but also fight against the tendency to fall into the traps it sets. These are all layered, complex, and multifaceted issues.

As the conversation intensified, J wrote,

> You have to be kidding me. You think I don't know we are slaves? That is one of our favorite amendments. Everybody on the conscious tip knows that amendment; it is like Prisoner 101. We acknowledge that our actions put us here and that we bear the primary responsibility for deserting our families, abdicating our responsibilities, and not being fathers, husbands, brothers, or sons. We consciously chose lifestyles that ensured that if we lost the game, we would buy into the whole complex— and worse. We just viewed it as the cost of doing business. What part don't you understand about that? What has that got to do with the Negroes, who would assist the slave master in keeping us corralled on the plantation? You woke up from that state of mind and

moved on from the uniform. Thousands of others are happy to be overseers. I'm supposed to excuse them 'cause they pay their mortgage, raise their kids, contribute to the economy, and pay taxes? Frankly, fuck 'em. They are doing what they feel is right and nothing that I think affects them. But don't tell me they aren't part of the enemy! Do you know what so-called terrorists say? 'There are no innocent people.'

If you support the system and benefit from its excesses and depredations, don't start crying when the car bomb goes off. I recently read an article in USA Today about a C.O. in Victorville who got stabbed 17 times and died. Am I supposed to be sad about that 'cause somebody finally snapped and attacked the closest symbol of the system they could get their hands on?

I couldn't fully embrace his belief that there were no innocent people. Such an extreme stance seemed too harsh for me. During my tenure as a correctional officer in the early 1990s, I encountered African American prisoners who shared J's values. They considered me a sellout and hurled derogatory epithets, accusing me of aiding "the White man" in their oppression, similar to the ideals J held. However, J forgave me, believing that I, too, had become conscious and politicized.

I am conscious of how the prison industrial complex harms people in favor of the rich. However, I did not see things as cut and dry as he did. Indeed, as a Black woman from the inner city now in the academic world, my standpoint has given me a broad lens through which to view intersections of power.

From my vantage point, it's essential to consider that many people who may seem aligned with the "enemy camp" are, in fact, casualties of the very institutions they serve. It's not a matter of us versus them but a collective struggle against an unjust system that impacts each of us differently. Should we disregard the fact that bank tellers, correctional officers, or city clerks are confined by economic necessities, societal expectations, and other constraints? Their roles within society should be considered alongside their personal battles or humanity. We must challenge the power structures and empathize with those entangled within them to effect systemic change. Assigning broad labels and classifications can breed isolation and division, inadvertently reinforcing the status quo. Not everyone is an adversary; many are simply surviving. The true enemy lies not in the individuals working within the system but in the system itself.

Despite my occasional perception of J as a cold piece of work, he proved to be more complex than I initially presumed. However, he was far from softhearted back then. In one of his emails to me, he shared the following thoughts:

> I have remorse for the individual tellers I ter-
> rorized, bank managers that I bulldozed, and
> ordinary people caught up in the scene be-
> cause I'm masked, gloved, openly armed,
> vaulting across counters, and laying people
> down. I imagine that is a genuinely traumatic
> experience for someone just coming in to cash
> their weekly paycheck and buy groceries for
> their family.

I now have to take a victim's impact class, and I know it's gon' be some bullshit. I listened to a few bank tellers talk about the trauma during the preliminary hearing. Some were devastated. I was usually non-abusive as long as you followed orders and laid your silly ass on the floor like I told you.

As I delved deep into J's political convictions, a thought nagged at me—did his politicization stem from a quest for power within prison walls and in the larger social sphere where the value of a Black man's life is diminished? Our debates on social justice were fierce. However, his proposed strategies to make the world more just often seem implausible.

Despite my reservations about the feasibility of J's strategies, I cannot deny their profound impact on my perspective. Engaging with his ideas and witnessing his unwavering dedication to activism pushed me to critically reevaluate my own assumptions. I immersed myself in documentaries and biographies that offer enthralling insights into the police, distributions of wealth and poverty, and racial justice. While our viewpoints did not wholly align, I deeply respected his commitment to fostering meaningful change.

§

When J was transferred to a federal penitentiary in Florida, I traveled from California to visit him. Our friendship had always been solid, and I eagerly anticipated a face-to-face conversation.

J entered the visiting room in standard-issue tan khakis, perfectly pressed and creased. He is thin and exceptionally tall, with long dreadlocks that flow like a river of rebellion and resilience, a tapestry of muted bronze and silver. Each strand is a story of resistance and survival. Sometimes, he exudes a muted reserve. During our Saturday conversation, I confided in him about the ill-fated attempt my best friend and I made to pursue a romantic relationship. J, always one to simplify everything, responded with his characteristic bluntness, saying, "Don't fuck your friends."

What truly tested my patience was J's persistent mispronunciation of my name. Despite my repeated corrections during our phone conversations, he continued pronouncing it as if it rhymed with "candy" instead of "Gandhi." While sitting across from him on our Sunday visit and after enduring one too many instances of being called "Nandy," I reached my breaking point. I impulsively hurled an entire deck of cards at him. Why is it so difficult for you to pronounce my name correctly? I flew across the country to visit him, yet this conscious brother would not give me my due respect by pronouncing the African name I had chosen for myself. The next hour was tense, and we labored to find enough words to fill the space. I left well before the 3 p.m. close of the visiting room, and it would be years before we spoke again.

§

J was released in 2009 after 18 years in prison. Today, he is a different man. The sharp edges of his youth have softened into wisdom. As a 68-year-old grandfather, he speaks to my students with humility and humor, sharing his story as a cautionary tale. He no longer clings to the rigid beliefs that once defined him, acknowledging that while systemic oppression is real, so is the power of individual transformation.

J initially found work as a house manager at a drug treatment facility. Although he sometimes felt like a correctional officer responsible for overseeing clients. He insisted that he always treated them with dignity. During his long bus rides home from work, he sometimes called me to share his discoveries of the latest technology, and I shared his joy. He had never walked miles to and from a job or taken the bus before his trip to prison, instead opting to own expensive vehicles and drive himself. Now, he prefers to spend his hard-earned money on his family.

J's journey from being a politicized prisoner to becoming a free man involved profound transformation and growth. His time in prison, marked by his firm beliefs and the impact he had on fellow inmates, had given him a sense of purpose and direction. However, after his release and reintegration, he fully grasped the broader implications of his beliefs, recognizing their potential limitations and harm. Adjusting to life outside prison, J embraces a more nuanced worldview that recognizes the importance of empathy, compassion, and understanding. As a 68-year-old with a calmer demeanor, professionally styled dreadlocks, and progressive views, J is now different from the person he was during his time as an O.G. in prison. His formerly polarizing views have mellowed, and he respects those who hold jobs and provide for their families, regardless of the nature of their work. He told me, "There's a purpose for that kind of thinking in prison, but it has no place in a truly free man's mind." He is a frequent guest speaker in my classes and even gave a TEDx talk. I'm uncertain if he ultimately embraced a deep understanding of the intersection between race and gender, though.

Mutulu "Doc" Shakur a free man on July 6, 2023. He was given a compassionate release when he became extremely ill with cancer. Jay was by his side during the last days.

§

In 2021, an exceptional artist adorned the streets of Philadelphia with two striking murals. One side of the busy road portrays J and fellow formerly incarcerated women and men dressed in standard prison uniforms, while the other depicts them in street clothes. The stark contrast serves as a poignant reminder of society's acceptance—or lack thereof—of the juxtaposition between prisoner and free.

Speaking of art, I was left breathless when I discovered a heartfelt surprise left on my doorstep back in 2005—a housewarming gift waiting for me on the move-in day when I bought my first house. It was a painting carefully crafted by J himself. It is an intricate masterpiece, an oil portrait of my face. The richness of my dreadlock's dances against a backdrop of vivid reds, vibrant yellows and oranges, and deep brown and black strokes. There is an unfiltered rawness to the painting. It was the centerpiece above the fireplace for seven years in that house, and now it is mounted above the couch in my current home.

I feel seen whenever I stand still in my living room and gaze at the painting. Every brushstroke, every minute detail carefully embedded on the canvas, resonates with one of my most profound love languages—acts of service. It showcases J's patience and devotion and is a profound testament to his affection for me. My guests are drawn to it, and I delight in sharing the story of my friend J, who immortalized my likeness from prison. The portrait is like a flower that bloomed in a concrete jungle, a ray of sunshine that emerged from a storm. The painting makes me feel radiant.

I feel beautiful.

WHEN THEY SPEAK ABOUT THEIR CHILDREN

Wounding and healing are not opposites. They're part of the same thing. It is our wounds that enable us to be compassionate with the wounds of others. It is our limitations that make us kind to the limitations of other people. It is our loneliness that helps us to find other people or to even know they're alone. I think I have served people perfectly with parts of myself I used to be ashamed of.

Rachel Naomi Remen

A colleague once shared that he lives fifty-one weeks every year, holding his breath for the one week in August when he can lose himself in the dust and delirium of Burning Man. I used to live something similar—not in the desert but in anticipation. I spent twenty-nine days a month waiting for one day to drive to the Leo Chesney Correctional Center. Nestled on an unassuming residential street in Live Oak, California, the now-abandoned, privately-owned, minimum-security prison was a place I once called my second home.

The first time I stepped through its gates was almost accidental. I tagged along with another sociology professor and her students, who were touring the facility. That's when I met Paula—initially the volunteer coordinator, later the warden, and eventually the town's mayor. As the tour ended, I lingered behind and found myself peeking into her office. "Do you think I could come back on my own?" I asked, half-hoping she'd laugh off the idea. Instead, her face lit up. Within two weeks, I was cleared to return, and for over a decade, that drive became ritual.

Every month from 2001 until 2012, I drove 40 miles in each direction. The institution closed in 2012 due to budgetary reasons. I facilitated deeply emotional conversations, outpourings of tears, first-time confessions, and strategies for living unencumbered in the free world. In that little room, surrounded by women who had lost so much, I gained something I didn't know I was looking for—a sense of purpose.

§

At annual volunteer appreciation events, as many volunteers gathered as there were prisoners housed at the facility. Most conducted Bible studies. Others assisted with filling out documents for social services or taught basic skills like applying for college financial aid. In truth, without these volunteers, the prison would have been nothing more than a warehouse for human pain.

Leo Chesney was run by the for-profit Geo Group, which charged the state roughly $39 per inmate per day when I began volunteering. By the time the prison closed, it had risen to $53. Overcrowding was the norm, with dormitories meant for fifty beds squeezed to accommodate far more. I resented the profiteering and the inhumane conditions, but if I'm honest, I was grateful for every extra woman who joined my sessions.

Throughout the years, I had the privilege of engaging with more than 1,000 women who came into my group sessions to bare their souls. Their experiences moved me to bring all the passion and compassion I could muster for an empowering message every month.

Over the years, more than a thousand women stepped into that room. Each carried her own weathered story, her own storm. Paula always introduced me as a motivational speaker, though I preferred to let the women decide if they felt motivated by the time I was done. The officers stopped escorting me after a while. "You know the way," they'd say, waving me off as though I were part of the institution itself.

Inside the education building, there was always a hum— a swirl of laughter, murmured catch-ups, and requests to Paula from prior attendees to return again. I often started with a clip from a motivational DVD played on an old bubble-back TV. But the heart of the sessions was conversation— raw, untamed, and transformative.

§

One activity I led was simple but revealing. I asked the women to imagine the room as a spectrum. At one end was

"Yes, that has been my experience," and at the other, "No, it hasn't." As they moved along the invisible line, answering questions about drug use, depression, violence, or abuse, a pattern emerged. Nearly every woman carried severe trauma, and many had also inflicted trauma in turn. Most were not violent offenders. They were survivors. And yet, what weighed heaviest wasn't the crime that brought them there—it was what they had left behind.

§

I met Tania in the group on a rainy winter day in 2003. She sat stiffly in her chair, arms crossed as if holding herself together. "My son's fourteen. He lives with my mom. I see him sometimes when I go to the mailbox, but we don't talk," she said, her voice brittle. I asked how she felt about that. She shrugged, insisting he was fine. "He's used to it," she added, though her eyes told a different story.

Barbara, another woman I'll never forget, had ten children, all born between short stints in county jail and prison. "The older ones know where I am, but I made them promise not to tell the younger ones," she said, her voice cracking with resolve. I urged her to reconsider. "Asking your kids to keep secrets from each other could hurt them more than the truth," I said gently. She stared at the floor, torn between protecting her children and confronting the damage already done.

"I understand your reasoning," I remarked, "but asking them to be secretive might do more harm than good. Reconsider what it means to ask your kids to keep secrets from each other."

"I think my babies are better off not knowing." Her gaze shifted to the floor. Could I dare speak of how these women should raise their kids from behind the walls? I've never been a mom or incarcerated. I turned to the others in the group, seeking their wisdom and support for Barbara.

§

I connected with the women around issues of motherhood and generational trauma. Although my mom did not abuse my brothers or me, like those I met at the Leo Chesney Center, she turned her trauma on herself and made choices that rendered her unavailable to us. Moreover, I never felt she was transparent about her life, like some women who came to my group. I am now middle-aged and hoping to fill in the gaps about who my mother was in the 1980s and '90s. Even though we connect on video chat daily, the topic instantly causes her to cry and check out.

§

Salena was a 52-year-old mom who found herself at the Leo Chesney Center in 2007, imprisoned on a warrant from 8½ years ago when she embezzled $10,000 from an accounting client. She told us she lived a life of opulence and excess, surrounded by live-in nannies and housekeepers who catered to her every whim. Her mortgage payments were a mere drop in the bucket, and she possessed a quarter-million-dollar watch that was given to her as a Christmas gift. Her children attended elite colleges, and politicians sought her accounting expertise. She reminisced about the taste of extravagance, the fine dining experiences in 5-star hotels, the expensive cars for her five children—and the husband's infidelity that ruined it all.

I asked Salena about her children's feelings, which she believed were based on her inability to pay their credit card bills and tuition while she was in prison. Rather than answering my question, she continued to list the accouterments of her privileged life, touching on her law school education, international travels, and the opulent wedding she had arranged for her oldest son.

I waited, then probed. "Salena, do you feel comfortable sharing how incarceration has affected your relationship with your kids?"

Her foot tapped the ground anxiously. "I don't give a damn. It's their cheating father they should be mad at."

She maintained that she gave her children everything and that her arrest on an old charge was frivolous. Given all she had done for them, "to hell with 'em" if they could not be patient with her during this short time. She motioned like she was throwing their partially read letters on the floor and said it was not her fault they were so rude.

§

In 2008, I met Tammy, a nineteen-year-old who kept her hands in the waistband of her bands. "When I was ten, I found my mom dead behind a liquor store," she said matter-of-factly, her arms folded tightly. By thirteen, she was selling drugs. "I don't even care that people died from the shit I sold them," she said, her voice cold and flat. "I don't even give a fuck, either." Her words were like a punch to the gut and left me speechless.

"That ain't even why I'm locked up. I never got caught for that," Tammy said, leaning back in the chair with her arms behind her head. I had never heard a more appalling story. It showed how a parent's choices could cause long-lasting effects of trauma on their child and society.

§

During another group session, an impeccably styled young woman named Lisa shared that she had called her 8-

year-old son earlier that day to wish him a happy birthday.

"How do you know it's my birthday?" he questioned.

She strained unsuccessfully to push back the avalanche of sadness. Her hands shook as she refused the half-roll of toilet paper offered by a woman behind her.

"I'm his mother." Her voice was barely above a whimper, and each word was sharply detached from the others.

The women's shame was intense. The guilt they felt about their crimes paled in comparison, as many contextualized their criminality as fueled by the disease of addiction, trauma, or a no-good man.

§

Janae was just 21 years old when I was invited to take her under my wing. Doing time for vehicular manslaughter, she earned only a three-year bid for killing an elderly woman while driving, infuriated at her boyfriend. She never uttered the words, "I killed someone." Instead, she frequently told disjointed parts of a tragic story, choked up by her apparent guilt.

Mr. Vidra, the starry-eyed counselor the women adored, implored me to look after Janae. "I don't know how to help this young woman. She needs you, Dr. Nandi," he nudged. "She is being eaten alive by her guilt. She's not ready to face her friends and neighbors, but she is paroling in a few months. I tried to convince her that she deserves a second chance."

Mr. Vidra escorted her to my workshop the first time, and she came independently every other time. The women were allowed to attend my monthly workshop only once during their stay, but Mr. Vidra gained permission from Paula to enable Janae to come as often as she wanted. Initially, she wore oversized denim pants and a white t-shirt that was standard issue. Her ensemble had ironed creases. Braces covered the top row of her teeth, and name-brand sneakers adorned her feet, both signs that someone in the free world was looking out for her. She had amazingly well-manicured cornrows, too, twisting and turning about her head.

She perched herself in the middle of the room among women old enough to be her mother. She stared at me fixedly in a manner that humbled me. When African American women saw that the speaker for the day was a Black female professor in her thirties, they often held a deep and penetrating gaze. Janae had a piercing look of admiration, and her eyes never strayed.

During the 2 p.m. break, when the other prisoners stepped outside to catch a whiff of open air and sun, Janae stayed inside with me. She scooted up next to me and talked freely about surviving rape at the hands of her stepfather. Janae asked if I thought she should tell her mother, and I replied that she should only if she believed her mom would be supportive. Then she showed me pictures of her three-year-old baby girl. Janae was guarded during the group conversations, but she sobbed when she pulled out the photograph of her daughter that she had tucked in her bra.

While still incarcerated, Janae wrote to me at the university numerous times. Each letter was sprayed with more perfume than the one before. Once, she began a letter saying, "I am bisexual." I presumed she wanted me to disclose my sexuality, but I did not want to engage Janae that way. I never replied to her letters because the institution's rules prohibited volunteers from corresponding with inmates. If I could have, I would have sent daily meditations, a list of affirmations to help her heal and forgive herself, and suggestions for activities to practice becoming a whole person again. I wanted to help her get free, whatever that meant for her. I wanted to utilize the space she carved out for me and teach her to be kind to herself.

Janae embraced too much guilt about "the accident" to confront the demons she carried. She reasoned that she deserved to be assaulted, punished, and scarred because of the pain she caused by killing someone. Ashamed of having earned such a brief prison sentence, she spoke in a muted, defeated voice, offering only curt responses to my questions.

She seemed resigned to her fate, resigned to living a life of suffering and regret. It was like she had given up on caring for herself. During her last month of incarceration, she arrived at the group wearing a mu-mu with a tattered collar. Only half of her hair was groomed. She hardly looked like the upbeat young sister I had met five months earlier. She refused to talk about her victim. Even though her release date was fast approaching, she didn't feel she deserved a second chance. I asked Janae about her plans after prison, but she shrugged and said she didn't know. "What about your daughter?" I pressed. I assumed she would have endless fun with her baby girl. She would never hang out with that no-good motherfucka' who got her into this mess in the first place. And she would always stay in touch with me.

I received a letter from Janae one week after her release in December 2009. She included a photo she had taken at a mall. Standing with her back to the camera, looking over her shoulder into the lens, her butt was squeezed into too-tight jeans. Her phone number was on the back under the words, "Having the time of my life." The number was not in service when I called.

I aspired to be more of a mentor than Janae desired. I

even thought of persuading her to visit the dead woman's gravesite and purge any distressing feelings she held by placing flowers, dancing a prayer, or simply being still. Janae would probably always avoid the site of the accident instead of confronting her innocence left there. She would undoubtedly manufacture excuses for always taking the long way to a cousin's house. Perhaps she would never mention the incident to her daughter when she started driving but instead bark at her for coasting 5 miles over the limit or staying out 20 minutes too late with the car.

Janae's story will not warrant compassion from most because many people will forever see her as someone who killed an elderly woman and served only three years for it. She was a foolish teenager, driving recklessly through the streets of central California to cuss out some man who had hung up the phone on her. But Janae is like many convicted people, who will castigate themselves more than a community or criminal record ever will. I fear she will spend the remainder of her life running from herself.

§

Evidently, no subject was more heartbreaking than the bond between a mother and her child. The children of these women suffered, but the mothers were not spared, either. While I never participated in similar groups with incarcerated men, I wonder if the emotions evoked are identical to those I witnessed in the groups I ran at the Leo Chesney Center. There, the women poured out their hearts, fears, and regrets. They cried and raged. We were all raw and vulnerable, holding nothing back. I helped them practice expressing remorse to their children and encouraged them to build healthy relationships in the future.

Many were caught in a vicious cycle of guilt and self-doubt, but I saw a lot of healing. They took the first steps toward personal growth, self-forgiveness, and rebuilding relationships with their children. I was profoundly affected by the emotions shared in the groups. I began to see my work as more than just a monthly volunteer commitment; it was a chance to genuinely impact the lives of women, their children, and perhaps generations.

At the end of each visit, Paula expressed heartfelt gratitude and assured me that the title "motivational speaker" she bestowed upon me was well-deserved. Despite the rule against physical contact, some women lined up for my hugs. Paula allowed it because she knew how much it meant to them, and I always had a hug for her, too.

§

In 2009 or 2010, amid the budget crunch in California, Paula told me there were plans to close the prison. Every week, a busload of women was transported back to the largest women's prison in the world, the Central California Women's Facility. During the months leading up to the closure of the Leo Chesney Center, the number of women attending my group sessions decreased from 12 to 15 people to 4-5. Just as I thought it was time to bid farewell, a state decision was made to keep it open. Busloads of women were transported back from central California to the small prison in the middle of a residential street. Once again, my group sessions were full. But in 2012, budget problems led to the facility's permanent closure.

As I turned to walk away from the prison for the last time, the sun was setting over the razor wire, casting long shadows across the grounds. I paused for one last look, taking in the fading light and the sight of the buildings, so stark and unforgiving against the darkening sky. At that moment, I felt the weight of all that had happened there—the triumphs, struggles, despair, and resilience. And, somewhere in the mix, my own growth. The prison had become more than a place of confinement; it was a place of rebirth. Prisoners turned their pain into purpose, and my life gained purpose, too.

Occasionally, while driving down Highway 99, I dip right and weave through the Live Oak neighborhood until I arrive at the baron building behind razor wire. From the sidewalk, I can see the window of the room where more than a thousand women I trusted each other, and we cried, laughed, took risks, and will likely never meet again.

FOOT SOLDIER

If you allow people to make more withdrawals
than deposits in your life, you will be out of
balance & in the negative.

Christie Williams

Josh sat in the front row every class, leaning in and
nodding rhythmically whenever I "went to chu'ch" on them.
Josh didn't look, talk, or move like the typical students in my
sociology classes. With his long shorts, knee-length white
socks, and hands covered in prison-quality tattoos, Josh
radiated something raw—an edge that made it clear he
wouldn't put up with anyone's bullshit. Not ever.

The year was 2012. Our class met on Tuesdays from 6:00 to 8:50 p.m. Six or seven weeks in, I requested that Josh hang back and chat with me. I caught Josh before he walked out, speaking over the commotion as students packed up.

"Hey, Josh."

"Yeah, what's up?" His head snapped up, and his eyes met mine. His expression was unreadable, though his eyes flickered with resistance.

After his classmates left, I said, "So, um, you're very vocal in class, and I noticed that we tend to agree on many issues. I'd like to know a bit more about you."

"Yeah, like what?" Josh's eyes scanned me from top to bottom, and his question suggested suspicion. This was my first hint that Josh never tells anyone more than they need to know.

"How long have you been a student here?"

"I've been going to school here off and on for a while. I'm gonna get shit right this time. Sorry for my language." Josh had heard me cuss plenty when I 'preached,' so I waved his apology away.

"I did some time. I just gave the state their number back, so I'm good now." He was off parole and completely free.

I nodded. "Really?" I was too eager, so I pulled back. "I appreciate you sharing that with me. How long have you been out?" It had been two years since his release, and he swore he was never going back.

We talked for nearly twenty minutes, our conversation interrupted only when the campus security officer reminded us that the building was closing. At just 5'3", Josh carried a presence that filled the room. He'd been a shot-caller for a white separatist gang, a man who navigated prison politics with the precision of a chess master. And yet, he insisted he wasn't racist.

"The politics in there are different," he explained. "You only associate with your own. That's just how it is."

In class, he was sharp, engaged, and often the first to challenge narrow thinking. I saw something in him—something more than his past.

§

Josh was once invited to join the notorious Nazi Low Riders (NLR). He was torn. It meant betraying the gang he had pledged his allegiance to for years. The NLR extended invitations solely to the most disciplined and resolute foot soldiers, creating a conflict between Josh's loyalty and the allure of joining a powerful organization. Whether exercising for hours daily, maintaining a pristine living space, trafficking drugs, or committing murder, foot soldiers are expected to obey. Josh's loyalty, however, was reserved exclusively for his comrades—the gang to which he had pledged his unwavering allegiance. Thus, despite the allure of becoming part of a dominant group like the NLR, there was no room for compromise.

I invited Josh to speak to my university students. His partner, Linda, came to campus with him, and I assured them of the friendly and respectful environment we had established. Still, Josh was guarded. The talk went well, and

§

Less than a year later, Linda sent me a message on Facebook: Josh had been arrested. My heart sank.

According to online arrest records, Josh had been pulled over, and the encounter escalated. He became agitated, fled on foot, and was eventually apprehended. Officers found over 35 grams of heroin and a fully loaded Smith and Wesson in his possession.

Shortly after his arrest, his father Mitch reached out to me, asking if I would visit Josh in jail. When I arrived, Mitch was waiting in the lobby. His face was lined with weariness.

"Josh talks about your class all the time," he said. "Thank you for being there for him."

When it was my turn to see Josh, I found him seated behind a plexiglass partition, clutching the phone with one hand. He looked relieved but ashamed.

"How are you holding up?" I asked.

"Well, I've been better." He leaned forward, his voice tight. "I need a favor, Nan'."

Josh explained his plan to sell his mobile home to cover legal fees. The buyer would give his dad the money, and I was to get it from him, hold onto to it for a few days, and pay the lawyer directly. "The rest is for my commissary if I end up doing time," he said. I agreed, feeling both honored by his trust and burdened by the responsibility.

§

The park where Josh's mobile home sat is on the north side of town, in a quaint neighborhood with a community center. Following Josh's suggestion, I drove by the house and found it ravaged. Broken furniture lay strewn about, floorboards ripped up as if someone had searched desperately for drugs or money. Linda had vanished, leaving remnants of her children's toys behind.

The new property owner paid Josh's dad $15,000, all 100-dollar bills. Mitch was aggravated as hell with his son, and he did not want the IRS to know he had that much money in cash. I headed to Mitch's mobile home park the day after the sale to collect the money. I was immediately greeted by twenty piles of Ben Franklin's face, crisp, turned in the same direction, spread across his vibrant red shag carpet. He instructed me to count the money, barely waiting for my acknowledgment before leaving the room. I towered over the spread, which was more cash than I had ever seen.

It was all there.

I called out to Mitch, informing him that I had finished counting the money. He brought me a sheet of lined paper to sign, acknowledging the ten thousand dollars in my possession. I requested an envelope and departed with Josh's money. My heart raced as I drove away.

I mailed the makeshift receipt to Josh, but when he called me, he said he trusted me and did not need proof of anything.

One week became two. Then three. Still, there was no private attorney. Josh had decided he would likely serve time and didn't want to waste the money on a losing case. The cash remained untouched beneath my mattress for several months. I felt honored that Josh trusted me with such a large sum of money, but I also carried the weight of responsibility on my shoulders. Whenever I thought about it, a knot of anxiety tightened in my stomach. I would regularly check beneath the mattress to ensure it was still there.

He was transferred from the local jail to the Sacramento County Jail, a couple of hours away. Per his request, I wrote a letter to the judge as his professor and spoke of his top-tier performance in my class. I also expressed that Josh had been grappling with addiction and had managed to clean up his act for a substantial amount of time.

The case escalated to the federal level, sparing Josh a third strike but sending him into a world where his reputation meant nothing.

In 2014, Josh wrote me a letter:

Hey, just to let you know, this place sucks! (haha) Seriously, I don't think I've ever experienced a worse program, not even in the SHU (secured house unit—solitary confinement). Yes, no joke, this place sucks. If possible, I should apologize or make amends, as I don't know if you're gaining any 'good sociology' from our interaction. I can't help but think about how our friendship seems to be all take on my end. Really, Nan,' I would have it be otherwise. Please express to me your thoughts on this, whatever they may be. I would sincerely like to know.

Collecting "good sociology" was the least of my concerns. I saw it as an opportunity to step up and help someone in desperate need. While I had previously assisted people in difficult situations, this was on a whole new level. Three months into his incarceration, I accepted the one-sided nature of our relationship, knowing that prisoners have limitations. However, I didn't anticipate becoming his foot soldier.

§

I drove to Sacramento for the court case the following year. I sat in the middle row, off to the right, as they escorted Josh from the holding area in an orange jumpsuit, handcuffed and chained. Judge Nunley, a middle-aged African American man, sentenced Josh to six and a half years in federal prison, unmoved by his claims of addiction and desire for a fresh start. After the verdict, Josh's public defender and I stepped outside, sharing our shared sense of disappointment. The attorney handed me personalized bracelets, crafted from jail-made string, with my name and others for Linda and her children. As I left the courthouse, I called Linda to break the news, realizing that six and a half years is a long time and expecting she wouldn't stick around.

Later that day, Josh called to express gratitude for my support in court. He had been having a tough time at Sacramento County Jail and requested a visit while awaiting transfer to prison. Despite the two-hour drive and the limited visiting hours, I agreed. He didn't have anything specific to tell me; he just desperately wanted to feel connected to someone safe.

Another prisoner visiting a loved one saw me and hinted to Josh that something was about to go down. Josh jerked his body toward him but held it together long enough to finish our visit. That night, Josh whipped his ass. As a white separatist, Josh was not supposed to associate with Black people.

On one occasion, I drove to the jail, circled the block until I found a parking spot near a 10-minute meter, and hurried inside. I planned to get on the visitation list and then return to move my car. However, after waiting in line, an officer informed me that Josh couldn't have any visitors, as he was in lockup for fighting. Frustrated, I returned to my car only to discover a $60 ticket for the expired parking meter. When Josh and I spoke later, he apologized for the inconvenience and told me to deduct the cost of the ticket from the cash I held for him. I don't remember if I did or not.

§

Over the next year, I continued to fulfill Josh's requests whenever he called or wrote. He often asked for books from Amazon, and I deposited chunks of his money into his prison account and ordered commissary packages for him.

Occasionally, he asked me to deposit funds into other prisoners' accounts. I didn't ask questions.

Foot soldiers never ask.

I also made deposits for Linda's kids, whom Josh considered his own. These deposits required trips to the U.S. Bank downtown. Linda had moved away and lived with her parents, who despised Josh. They allowed her to stay with them, but only if she avoided all contact with him. Despite being in her 40s, Linda relied on her parents. They threatened to take custody of her children when they caught her on the phone with Josh. She eventually ended her relationship with him, but not before I followed orders to give her over a thousand dollars throughout the year, including funds for bills, Christmas presents, and helping her find her own place.

I printed the financial breakdown of his cash and mailed it to him. At first, I sent spreadsheets to prove my trustworthiness, but Josh assured me he believed me.

"If you tell me the money is gone, I'll believe you. No need to send any proof of how you spent it." I was his "homegirl," he proclaimed. "I trust you, Nan'."

I kept receipts at first, fearing his reaction if he thought I'd stolen from him. Later, I became exhausted and simply tucked banknotes and Amazon screenshots into the pages of a book I was reading or the side pockets of my backpack. Although frustrated and overwhelmed, I was always mindful of the potential consequences of crossing him.

After Josh's money was depleted, his phone calls from prison became infrequent. That was fine with me. In one of his emails, he invited me to ask him anything, but he was guarded with his words. He emailed and called me between trips to the hole for fighting but never mentioned the cause of those fights. Josh never spoke about who started what, the extent of the pain he inflicted, who authorized the hit, or what happened afterward. He only wanted to share his pain over Linda ending things.

At one point, he told me about his refusal to "cell up" with a Black man. "That's not how I do my time," Josh told me in response to why he was in the hole for refusing to live with a Black man.

In the general population of California state prisons, where Josh racked up most of his time, prison politics dictate that White men live only with other White men—unless those White men are sex offenders, in which case most people don't want to cell up with them. Although federal prisons have more lax racial codes, Josh was still only willing to live with other Whites. I reiterated that the environment was different, and I nudged him to be true to his principles of being non-racist.

"You aren't the same person you were when you did time before." I had hoped I was right.

"I hear you, Nan'."

"What's the big deal? Do what the officers tell you to do. This is not a California mainline. Just accept the cellmate they give you." He refused and was sent to segregation for his stubbornness.

Despite being intrigued by his various ways of advocating for justice in my class and on social media, I never probed Josh too much about his involvement in white supremacy or prison politics. Josh was simply conforming to the politics prevalent among the general population. I guess. I didn't know if he genuinely held negative views toward people of color, but he always treated me respectfully.

§

Josh contacted me sparingly during the final year of his six-year confinement. He was often in the hole for incidents, which he referred to only in vague terms. Josh was most likely insubordinate to officers, had dirty urine samples, or beat someone's ass. Over time, the requests piled up. Money for Linda's kids, for Josh's commissary, for books, for God knows what else. I stopped keeping track of how much I'd given. When his money ran out, he began asking for mine. Each time, he promised to pay me back—next week, next month, as soon as his "homeboy" came through. I wanted to believe him.

"Hey Nan', I'm trying to stay focused. They have a leather-making program here, but I have to rent a locker to store all my materials. If I could, um, borrow $75, I promise I'll get it right back to you as soon as my homeboy gets paid." "I've been playing in the band, but I need _____." I swear I will pay you as soon as my brother gets paid next week." "I know I owe you, but if you don't mind sending me _____, I promise to get it right back to you." Through stutters and promises stacked on top of one another, Josh had a lot going on.

During our conversations, Josh's emails were well articulated, but his phone calls included many odd pauses and fillers. His tone was more determined and pitched higher than when he described his disdain for prison. He assured me he was trying to get his life on track, despite loathing the prison environment and wishing it were more like the state system.

Once, Linda called me to vent. It had been a while since they had spoken, but she was still curious about how he was doing. I told her he was okay but had been asking me for money. "He's on drugs again," she said. Although it shocked me, I wasn't entirely surprised. When I emailed Josh to confirm, he became angry and expressed disappointment. He didn't explicitly deny Linda's claim, but I didn't hear from him again for a year. He remained upset with me until he wrote to me in September 2019 from solitary confinement.

A month after I received that letter, I answered a call from an unknown number. It was Josh informing me that he had been released from the federal penitentiary earlier that day. He had returned to southern California to be near his mom, stepdad, and brother. However, Josh's brother, who owned a commercial painting company and had employed him before, became unsupportive due to Josh's multiple prison trips. This strained their relationship, and his brother's advice to their mom to be careful of him made her reluctant to assist him in getting back on his feet. Thus, he needed me again.

Required to stay in a halfway house for 90 days, Josh told me he could leave if he had a job lined up. He said his brother's friend was willing to take a chance on him, but he needed his own industrial sprayer. Josh sold his watch for $40, but that was not enough.

"Any chance you can send me $200? As soon as I get this sprayer, I can get a job and get out of here. My homeboy gets paid next week, and I can have him bring it to you." Josh claimed there was a holdup at the halfway house, so he had to do the entire 90 days. Then he needed underwear, work clothes, and shoes for the painting gig waiting for him the second he was out of there. I mailed cash to the facility twice so he could get what he said he needed.

By the end of September 2020, exactly one year after his release from custody, Josh had returned to northern California and lived just three miles away from me with his dad. He assured me that he was committed to repaying the money he owed me. I had stopped keeping track of the amount long ago, and instead, I proposed that he paint rooms in my home to settle our debt. Painting is a chore I despise. Initially, Josh promised to start the job promptly, but as days passed, his promises failed to materialize. He repeatedly called with excuses, often using his father as an excuse. He only showed up twice, despite planning to be here every day for three weeks. It was evident to anyone entering my house that a paint job was underway, with rearranged furniture and drop cloths covering the floor. In response to each call and text, I simply replied with a non-committal 'Okay.'

Eventually, he came. But after painting only two walls of my home office in almost a month, he texted another excuse for why he could not finish that last day. I responded with the following text:

> I will finish what you started. It has been a roller coaster, and I have scheduled my days around your commitment to be here. It is more frustrating than rewarding, and you've bailed more than you've shown up. Grab your ladder and supplies whenever you can. I need to keep things moving because my brain feels out of sorts with your shit all over my house. My Airbnb guests' comfort is essential, and my frustration level is too high at this point. I appreciate your work, but I'm ready to call it quits.

Within an hour, Josh was at my front door. He didn't say hello. Instead, he stormed through my living room and out the back door, where I had placed his brushes and bucket.

After grabbing his items, he headed back toward the front door but stopped short.

"I was going to get this done, but things kept springing up." His voice was tight with emotion. "I'll come back tomorrow and finish before I start my new job."

"Nah, I'm good. I appreciate the offer, but I think it's best to call it quits." The promises were too much.

Josh's expression softened briefly with a hint of remorse. He turned away from me and walked out the door. Later, he posted a cryptic Facebook message about regret and losing someone close, and I wondered if it might have been about me. At that moment, I decided to no longer be available to Josh should he find himself in trouble with the law again.

Fool me once—.

§

Shame on me.

At the beginning of 2022, he stopped posting regular updates to Facebook. Curiosity got the better of me, so I searched the local jails to see if he might be in custody. Unsurprisingly, he was back at the Sacramento County Jail. I should have clicked away from the page and focused my energy on chores or homework. Instead, I clicked on "send email" and expressed concern for his circumstances and safety.

Josh called me the next day. He said his parole officer sent federal agents to arrest him after he provided a third positive urinalysis while on parole. Josh was furious and felt he deserved drug treatment, a second chance, or anything other than jail time. He was sentenced to eight months in jail.

From Sacramento County Jail, Josh wrote to me at the university, acknowledging our one-sided relationship once again. He said he felt terrible that I had always been there for him despite his inability to give me anything in return. He promised to help with whatever I needed as soon as he was out of jail. The commitment I'd made to myself fell by the wayside. When he is locked up, he is kind. I respond well to kindness, so I began to help again.

"I just want you to paint my house, Josh," I replied, hopeful but reserved.

"You got it, Nan'," he said. I wanted to believe him.

Josh was transferred to the Colusa County Jail due to overcrowding in Sacramento. Scheduled for release in September 2022, he called me on a late Friday afternoon in the middle of summer to ask for another big favor. The probation officer mandated a drug treatment program that he would have to pay for. Josh had $2500 in his inmate account at the Colusa County Jail and needed it to disappear before his release date. He asked me to come as soon as I could.

On Monday morning, I drove an hour to collect Josh's money. As he had said, a check was waiting for me at the front desk. I brought it home, where it sat until he began sending instructions to buy books from Amazon. From that time until the day of his release three months later, Josh called me at least once a week to ensure that everything was fine.

As his discharge date approached, staffing issues threatened his ability to depart at 12:01 a.m., as someone at the jail had assured him he could. His departure might not happen until after 3 p.m., and that was unacceptable to him. Josh called to ask if I would contact headquarters and insist he be let go at 12:01 a.m. With no intention of demanding anything, I called the jail and spoke to an exasperated officer, at whom Josh had allegedly yelled about his departure time.

"Hi, I was calling to get information about Josh, who is scheduled to be released tomorrow."

She declared she was doing all she could to make it happen but could no longer deal with him screaming at her. I knew she was telling the truth.

"I'm sorry, ma'am. Thank you so much."

A friend picked him up from the jail at 12:01 a.m. and drove him to my house. An hour after he was released, Josh knocked on my front door. He wanted his money in cash, so I placed 100s, 50s, 20s, 5s, singles, and coins in an envelope with an itemized breakdown of what I spent on his commissary and books. I also included a note of good luck. We exchanged hugs in the driveway, and I said I would wait for him to finish drug treatment so he could paint rooms for me.

I did not hear from him until December, when he called to ask for $750 to get a room at a sober living facility. He initially had enough for a nice place, but when he arrived there, they went through his inventory, told him his methadone prescription disqualified him, and said he was not welcome to stay.

"That's too steep for me, Josh." I was sure loaning him $750 would leave me high, dry, pissed off, and blowing up his phone. Two weeks later, he sent a text message, claiming he was only short $200 for a different sober living house.

> I hate to bother you, but I'm down $200. That's all I'm short. As for the painting, it'll have to wait until I'm in the program. My probation officer ordered me to stay at my friend's house until I get into a sober living place. I even asked her about doing some work for you to

help get the money together, and she said it would be cheating Social Security. I get my $1100 social security check on the 30th because the first falls on a weekend, and I will immediately return the $200. I know it's an imposition, and I'm sorry.

The left corner of my mouth curled upward. On the one hand, if Josh genuinely wanted to get help with his addiction, I was down to help. But the idea that he couldn't work for me because he would be cheating Social Security was bullshit. Still, I relented because I figured there was no way he would use the money on drugs, knowing he would earn himself a one-way ticket back to prison.

"I can loan it to you, but I need a commitment that you will return my money on the 30th." Would the loyalty he showed his friends in prison be extended to me, too?

"I absolutely will, Nan. You have my word," he texted.

Josh texted me his CashApp name, and I sent him $200.

Just minutes before noon on the day he was due to pay me back, I sent him a text that merely read, "Hey, Josh."

He replied, "Hey, Nan. I haven't forgotten. As soon as it's here, I'm CashApp'n."

At about 5:00 p.m., I texted again. "Any updates?"

I did not need the money. Instead, I wanted him to show me that he respected my generosity. I deserved to feel appreciated. Mostly, though, I wanted to not feel like a fucking fool.

"It'll be just a few minutes, Nan." His tone implied I was getting on his nerves.

Immediately, he sent a photo of two $100 bills on a black table with a torn sheet of bank letterhead in the background.

"I have the money. But I have to deposit it back into the

bank to use CashApp. They only allow three transactions a day on my temporary debit. But if the guys here are okay with it, I'll try at midnight. But that money will get to you. Thank you again for your help."

I was fidgety and annoyed. How come paying me back was not one of the three transactions Josh made that day? Why wasn't I a priority—not just this time, but every time he was free to make choices about repayment?

At about 11 p.m., he sent me $199 on CashApp and a text message that read, "I'm a dummy, but I need to give them $201 for you to receive $200. No, thank you. I still owe you a buck."

From when Josh was released in September 2022 until the middle of January 2023, I asked him to paint for me three or four times. He will, he insisted, as soon as he completes the rehabilitation program. He will—as soon as he gets settled into the halfway house. He will. Just not right now.

At the end of January, I sent another message telling him I would do the painting myself, as it seemed like I was begging. He responded that he would do it that weekend. On Friday, he called and asked if I wanted him to come immediately to see what work needed to be done.

"Yes, I do."

He was confident that every wall I wanted him to paint could be done in a day, so he changed course seconds after his offer to do an assessment, indicating that he would just call me from outside my front door at 10 a.m. Saturday. I could hear apathy in his voice; his words were stammered, and his low tone was familiar.

"Uh, I will just get it knocked out tomorrow. My buddy's going to let me use his tools, so you don't have to buy anything. It doesn't sound like there is much to do." He sounded uninterested, and I wasn't even sure I wanted him in my house.

On Saturday, I received a phone call from Josh at around 10:30 a.m. When I picked up, I asked, "Are you outside?" I already knew he wasn't.

He explained that he was waiting for a friend to arrive so he could borrow his roller and brushes and that he would keep me updated. I knew better than to base my entire day around Josh's promises, but I headed to Lowe's and purchased the paint anyway.

By 1:30 p.m., Josh called again to say that his friend still had not shown up but would do the work the next day and be at my house at 9 a.m. At 9:30, Josh messaged that he was leaving his house and heading in my direction. An hour later, he sent a text message explaining that his car had broken down on the side of the road and he was waiting for a friend to pick him up. I suspected that Josh had not even gotten out of bed yet. He would have told me where he was and asked me to pick him up if he was actually stranded.

I was not nearly as upset as I had been a couple of years prior when he pulled the same stunt. It was clear that he did not see his connection to me as sacred; he was not the least bit loyal. This is why friends and family members frequently give up on their incarcerated loved ones. Their assurances are robust and sincere until they return to the free world. They repeatedly disappoint and fail to follow through.

My "friendship" with Josh taught me a lot about setting and sticking to boundaries, even when faced with emotional tugs at my heartstrings. In October 2023, Josh was arrested again on drug charges. Less than a month later, a letter arrived at my home, a confession of his shortcomings as a friend. He offered an apology and then requested lyrics for several songs. Suspecting that this simple task was a ploy to draw me back in, I sent nothing. Initially, I considered seizing the opportunity to pen a lengthy letter to express my feelings. However, before I could put pen to paper, another letter arrived from the jail, urging me to respond— even if it meant telling him to "fuck off." His desperation was palpable. Staring down the barrel of a third strike and a 25-to-life sentence, he was isolated without support from his disenchanted family or unreliable friends. My silence echoed loudly. He stood alone.

I will never again be his financial crutch. His calls to me will go unanswered, and his letters will gather dust. The ties between us have severed. For the next 25 years, he must seek reliance from the next unsuspecting soul.

My feet hurt.

SOLITARY

I have not been able to reach out and physically touch another human being since I was first tossed into solitary confinement in the county jail 14 years ago—just ten days after my initial arrest. These cops and prison guards touch me all the time to put handcuffs and chains on me or, once in a blue moon, to beat or assault me. But I have been unable to touch anyone else, even with hugs.

I tried to remember what touching another person with my fingertips, not my fists, actually felt like, but I could no longer remember. I recently spent about an hour touching my own arm. I tried to block out the sensation of being touched on the skin by focusing solely on what my fingertips were feeling, hoping to remember what it felt like to touch another person. But I couldn't quite disconnect from touching my arm enough to achieve the sensation I was looking for. So, I finally stopped trying.

Justin, 2010

Justin's words from his letter haunted me. By the time I read them, he had already spent 14 years in solitary confinement. The depth of his isolation was unfathomable, even with the details he shared. His life inside Colorado State Penitentiary (CSP)—a facility designed to keep 725 prisoners in complete isolation—was featured in a National Geographic documentary that first introduced me to his story. Men at CSP had no access to outdoor exercise, no chance to interact with one another, and no opportunities to learn skills for reintegration into the general population, let alone the outside world. In solitary confinement, existence itself is reduced to survival in a concrete box.

In the NatGeo film, other prisoners discussed the horrors of solitary. They described it as torture. Hearing the screams of fellow prisoners suffering from severe mental health issues due to their isolation, Justin confirmed that these reports were not exaggerations.

In the film, Justin sat restrained by cuffs and a waist chain, officers hovering tensely at his sides. His light skin, thick glasses, and ponytail gave him an air of quiet intellect, but his muted eyes betrayed a life drained of vitality. Despite the hovering officers, his voice was steady, his tone calm, as he described a system designed to break him. He had not felt the wind on his skin in 14 years. That detail alone was enough to break my heart.

A profound sense of despair shrouded me as I read Justin's letter. The hopelessness conveyed in his words as he explained enduring 14 years of utter isolation was awful to imagine. Yet I knew that the reality was even worse. I felt powerless in the face of such suffering, but I offered what comfort I could. I assured him that I had heard him, and I extended a bridge of connection.

He sent letters more frequently than I did. His were long, detailed, and handwritten, squeezed between the faint lines on both sides of the paper. Mine were often typed, focused on the essentials of my day-to-day life. In our moments of shared vulnerability, he sometimes spoke of his childhood in southern California as a cheerful kid with parents and sisters. I read his letters with a heavy heart, as they often centered on the pains of loneliness and the injustices of his confinement. I never shared my phone number, so the sound of his laugh is still a mystery.

§

Justin's defiance, both in life and in confinement, was a defining thread in his story. Early in his time at CSP, he found himself in trouble for reasons he couldn't fully explain. The documentary captured one incident where he refused to leave the dayroom after his allotted one-hour recreation period. Ignoring orders to "cuff up," he tied his socks together, placed them over his nose to prepare for pepper spray, and tucked his arms inside his shirt to make himself harder to restrain. The standoff ended without violence, but when I later asked him why he had resisted, he simply shrugged. "I didn't have a reason."

Prisoners at Colorado State Penitentiary earn privileges

by maintaining an infraction-free record while advancing through a six-point ranking system known as the Quality-of-Life Program, where compliance was rewarded and resistance punished. Benefits such as television and phone calls can be granted or revoked based on the prisoner's behavior. Level one is the most stringent, and men on the first step are allowed only a two-hour non-contact visit per month. The program was modeled after the core principles at Eastern State Penitentiary (ESP), an infamous gothic structure developed by Quakers over 180 years ago. ESP was designed to foster "true" penitence; inmates were isolated in their cells with only a skylight, symbolizing a direct line to a deeper relationship with God. According to the neuropsychologist in the documentary, instead of becoming penitent, most of them "simply went mad."

A former CSP warden in the documentary remarked that the facility operates very close to the boundaries set by the U.S. Constitution regarding cruel and unusual punishment. If a prisoner is entitled to three 5-minute showers per week, CSP ensures each man gets exactly three 5-minute showers per week—no more and no less.

Justin often portrayed his struggles as deliberate attempts by the staff to induce psychological disorders, such as antisocial personality disorder, paranoia, compulsive outbursts, depression, and post-traumatic stress disorder. He feared psychotropic medications would dull his senses, forcing him to submit. He often referred to himself as a product of the system, a creation of the Colorado Department of Corrections. He believed that the prison's administrators had deliberately pushed him toward mental illness, their goal being to reduce him to a docile, compliant inmate. Justin was anything but. He believed that he had endured every type of injustice, including being mocked by the system, American citizens, his own family, and even viewers of National Geographic.

While I don't know if there was a deliberate conspiracy to demean him, depriving individuals of social interaction substantially affects their brain chemistry, emotional growth, and mental health. Consequently, the jailers expect compliance and obedience. Subjecting people to long periods of solitary confinement can make them docile, not because they become self-aware and penitent, but because they have been subjected to extreme psychological distress that breaks them down. Alas, many people become more, not less, aggressive.

Before prison, Justin had never considered himself violent. Yet years of isolation had reshaped him into someone he barely recognized. In one letter, he confessed to punching two correctional officers without provocation, admitting that he didn't even know their names. "I don't do well with people anymore," he wrote. I struggled with how to respond. Part of me wanted to offer understanding, to tell him, "I get it." But I didn't, not fully. It wasn't until my relationship with Justin that I began to see the humanity behind the rage of men confined to segregation. Their outbursts, vulgarities, and defiance were not random acts of aggression—they were the language of desperation.

§

Justin shared with me the details of his legal case and the testimonies at the core of his initial 14-year sentence. I researched the documents and scrutinized the signed reports written by the arresting officers after his 1996 apprehension. I compared them with court transcripts available online.

Unsurprisingly, the discrepancies between the officers' initial accounts of a scuffle and their defense were glaring.

On September 4, 1996, officers orchestrated a quasi-sting operation to apprehend Justin while he attempted to sell computer equipment in a store. The plain-clothes detectives stood behind him while he waited for the employee to come back with an estimate. To Justin's surprise, the two unidentified men told him he was under arrest on suspicion of stolen goods. When they attempted to detain him, a scuffle ensued. Justin believed that random men claiming to be officers attacked him.

Later, it was determined that the computer equipment was not stolen. Thus, his criminal trial was centered on assaulting the cops.

At the trial, and in dramatic Hollywood fashion, the District Attorney stated that Justin "went on the attack" while the officers were simply performing their duties. His opening statement was the following:

> You are going to hear that he grabbed at Detective Hatfield. You are going to hear he did it to hurt—just like he kicked Detective Grahn to hurt him. What you are going to hear is that Justin did not grab at Detective Grahn's knees, did not grab at Detective Hatfield's neck, did not grab at Detective Hatfield's waist, his shoulders, or his head. What you are going to hear is that Justin went for the throat. And when he did, he grabbed Detective Hatfield's tie and twisted it, making the knot tight at his throat. And you are going to hear that that was in an attempt to choke him.

The judge then asked Justin's public defender if he wanted to make an opening statement. He replied, "No."

Officer Hatfield's initial report states that Justin "tried to pull away" and was "forced to the ground," after which he "attempted to kick" and "attempted to bite" Officer Hatfield. The arrest report mentions no other injuries or assault attempts. However, while on the witness stand, Officer Hatfield described the altercation as Justin choking him despite no such statement being recorded immediately following the incident. Detective Grahn's written account specified that only his hand and elbow were wounded during the arrest. But during his court testimony, Detective Grahn said he feared for his life and believed Justin would kill him. "I could think of nothing but my family and whether I would make it home that day."

Justin had been a fugitive from California after escaping a juvenile detention facility a year prior. The arrest warrant suggested that he might be armed, which may have justified the detectives' use of force during his apprehension. This same fact could have also influenced the jury to perceive him as more combative than he actually was. Justin assured me that he did not resist the arrest, but he likely defended himself against unfamiliar men who falsely accused him of a crime he did not commit.

Justin's attorney offered no closing statement. He was convicted on two counts of second-degree assault against the officers. Justin is now ineligible for a parole hearing until he reaches the age of 85 in 2060 due to the additional time added to his sentence while in solitary confinement. The CDOC website states his mandatory release date is February 7, 2128. Justin was placed in isolation ten days after his arrest, where he sat for many years before and after I became his pen pal.

His case is fraught with numerous challenges, including inadequate legal counsel, rejected appeals, dismissed class-action lawsuits, multiple instances of mistreatment, and a prison sentence that seems to lengthen each year. Under these conditions, it's no surprise that he rejects all notions of justice that the Colorado Department of Corrections puts forth. At various stages of his original case and subsequent appeals, Justin unsuccessfully acted as his own attorney.

§

In his letters to me, he frequently poured out his emotional strife, describing the hardships he endured at the hands of what he believes to be racist and sadistic correctional officers. His despair was palpable in every letter. Convinced that the CDOC was profiting from his incarceration, he argued that confining him to a high-security facility brought additional financial gain for the state. While it is true that companies profit from commissary sales and inmate phone calls, solitary confinement places a significant financial burden on the state. A 2020 report published on the Colorado Department of Corrections website reveals that it costs taxpayers an astounding $164.94 per day to house, feed, supervise, and provide medical treatment for each of the 725 men at CSP. This equated to over $60,369 per year. Thus, Justin's belief that the state profits from his imprisonment is a misconception, as the financial burden on taxpayers to sustain high-security facilities like CSP is substantial. Recognizing the economic implications introduces an additional layer of complexity to the challenges experienced by both incarcerated people and the state.

While the financial costs are significant, they are

outweighed by the emotional, physiological, and social damage inflicted upon individuals who endure years of isolation. In the documentary in which I first saw Justin, a man spoke about their repetitive back-and-forth pacing from the bunk to the door, sometimes for hours each day, creating grooves in the concrete floor. This particular scene in the film is so gut-wrenching that I occasionally share a brief clip of it in my Prison Industrial Complex class to demonstrate the anguish of solitary confinement. Being intrinsically social creatures, humans experience a gradual unraveling of the mind when deprived of interpersonal contact. Extensive periods of solitude result in anxiety, depression, and, in severe cases, hallucinations or psychotic episodes. Justin wrote about sleepless nights haunted by nightmares and waking hours overshadowed by a distorted sense of reality.

The warden's stance on solitary confinement was that it's a "time out" that allows men to reset and cultivate a deeper understanding of themselves and their behaviors. However, this contrasts with extensive research by a neuropsychologist in the film who said prolonged isolation impacts the brain region responsible for processing pain.

Before his imprisonment, Justin had never regarded himself as violent. In one of his letters, he expressed pent-up rage and a deep desire for revenge against prison staff and administrators who had caused him much pain and suffering. Without provocation, Justin once impulsively punched two officers whose names he didn't even know because now he "doesn't do well with people." I wasn't sure how to support him with his violent impulses, although I sometimes wanted to say, "I get it." I didn't use to get it, though. Men in the segregation unit at the Annex who yelled vulgarities from the slits in their cell doors made my job extremely unpleasant. Based on what I learned through my relationship with Justin, their behavior made sense.

Alongside his anger aimed at the prison staff, Justin wrestled with grief. He had been deeply in love with a woman who was his pen pal, and they were engaged to be married. Despite the countless hours she devoted to advocating for him, Justin exploded in fury when she refused to follow through on one last task and then did not contact him for months. In his correspondence, Justin shared his perspective on how the loss of normalcy in relationships was yet another cruel consequence of long-term isolation.

Driven by curiosity, I searched online and stumbled upon a MySpace page Justin's fiancé had set up for him. On May 21, 2009, at 5:19 a.m., she set the status to "There is nothing more I can do. I'm sorry." The mood was "exhausted." The anguish reflected in her online presence mirrored Justin's agony, reinforcing the impact of isolation on both sides of their relationship.

§

In 2010, I communicated with his younger sister, Melinda, via Facebook. He had told me her first name in a letter, and I searched it alongside his last name and found a woman who bore a striking resemblance. I messaged, asking, "Any chance you have a brother named Justin?"

Within a day, she replied, "It's strange that you should contact me now. He has been on my mind a lot lately."

"Are you down to chat with me on the phone?" I waited a half-day for a reply.

"Sure," she said.

During our discussion, she revealed that Justin's history of challenging authority began in their childhood. She described a photograph from their early years. Their mom explained the story behind the photo as Justin's defiance in refusing to put his arm around his baby sister despite their mother's insistence. She also reminisced about a frigid winter day in middle school when Justin carried her on his back for the remaining four blocks home after she had complained of aching, freezing feet. Among her recollections, this stood out as one of her fondest memories of him.

As Melinda recounted memories of their childhood, sadness colored her voice. She also conveyed shock at seeing him on NatGeo, still confined to solitary after all the years since her last visit with him. But she agreed with the state's decision to keep Justin locked up, fearing he would get into trouble again if he were released. She did not, however, like that he was still in isolation. I pictured Melinda's face, pale and strained.

Melinda and Justin's dad had died two years before my conversation with her, and Justin did not know. I offered to break the news to him, and she said that would be best. As I composed the letter, I wondered how he would react and whether he would feel distraught about not having been closer to his father before his passing. Grief is complicated, and the death of a parent can be difficult to process, even for the estranged. I signed the letter with an earnest message and sent it off with a prayer. Indeed, Justin expressed that there was no love lost.

§

In a sobering letter a couple of years after we began corresponding, Justin beautifully described his newest joy, which tugged at me in every direction. Assigned to a different facility to work levels 4, 5, and 6 of the Quality-of-Life Program, he found himself in a new cell with narrow, vertical windows, each barely five inches wide and close to the ground. Across multiple pages, he wrote about a shrub visible through the narrow window of his new cell. The shrub, just 18 inches from his fingertips, was the closest he had been to a living plant in 15 years. He described its leaves changing from green to gold, the bugs scurrying at its base, and the way life seemed to unfold just beyond his reach. The irony of being so close to nature, yet completely cut off from it, was not lost on him—or me. It was both a reminder of the world he had lost and a cruel taunt from the universe.

§

Over the years, Justin's requests grew overwhelming. He asked me to research his case, contact people on his behalf, and send him materials ranging from maps to fish species. I once spent an entire afternoon printing and organizing maps, only to learn that they had been confiscated because maps posed a security risk. His disappointment was palpable in his next letter, and I found myself questioning whether I could keep up with the demands of our correspondence.

Eventually, I stopped writing.

Two years later, when I finally sent him a letter, I immediately sensed the toll time had taken on his mental health from his return letter. As if squeezing a dissertation into just eight pages, he shared extensive strategies to have a saltwater aquarium in his cell, hoping to sell the fish and earn money. He asked me to contact aquatic wholesalers and provide him with information on assorted plant and fish species. I did, but then I stopped writing.

§

Amid the pandemic, when the world was isolating, I searched Justin's name online and found the Avid Prison

Project webpage. In a four-minute video, he shared a fragment of his story. As the camera panned his cell, I recognized a blurred photograph of myself hanging among pictures of his family. It had been five years since we last communicated. My heart ached at the thought of all the time that had passed, but I also felt a warm glow of gratitude, knowing that our correspondence had meant something to him.

§

During the National Geographic program in which I learned about Justin, I also saw Josue. He was at CSP for the second time. In his interview, Josue drew a parallel between his circumstances and the character played by Tom Hanks in the movie Castaway. "That guy was talking to a volleyball." Reflecting on his own experience, he acknowledged the detrimental effects of five years spent devoid of any human connection. The first time he was discharged, he was given no assistance or resources to facilitate successful reintegration into society. As the credits rolled, Josue exited the prison gates into the loving arms of his family. I wondered how long it would take him to behave erratically in a partnership or with a stranger and when he would be in prison again.

Justin and Josue have been reduced to mere cogs in America's relentless system of incarcerating people in segregation. Considering the staggering daily expense of $165, there are countless avenues through which this taxpayer investment could have been channeled to support their rehabilitation and personal development. Mentorship, vocational training, higher education, therapy, spiritual guidance, anger management programs, and innovative approaches like animal-assisted therapy could have equipped them with the tools required for self-reliance and success both during incarceration and upon release.

He and 22 other inmates at the facility attempted to bring a class action lawsuit against the Department of Corrections because CSP lacked an outdoor exercise area. Interestingly, conservative Supreme Court Justice Neil Gorsuch was one of the judges in his appeals case, which focused mainly on his ability to pay court costs associated with filing the complaint at the CDOC. Pre-release and academic programs have been added at CSP since the last time Justin and I connected, and construction for outdoor recreation areas began in 2016.

§

Solitary confinement is utilized in prisons beyond Colorado, with segregation units found in most correctional facilities and 31 supermax prisons dispersed nationwide. Many people confined to supermax prisons exhibit violent tendencies and pose considerable management challenges if placed in the general inmate population. The issue of managing unruly prisoners has been a longstanding and contentious topic, and I do not claim to have solutions.

Solitary confinement is a feature of prisons across the United States, with over 31 supermax facilities housing men like him. These are men deemed too dangerous or unruly for the general population, their lives reduced to a cycle of isolation and punishment. And yet, research has shown that prolonged solitary confinement often exacerbates the very behaviors it is meant to correct. It strips people of their humanity, leaving them angrier, more broken, and less capable of reintegration.

§

Solitary

In a documentary about Red Onion State Prison in Virginia, a man described the psychological toll of isolation. "You've got to feel like you're relevant to somebody," Michael said. "If you don't feel relevant to anyone, it'll make you want to lose your damn mind." His words echoed Justin's letters, where he described the pain of being unseen, unheard, and forgotten.

In speaking to the producers of the show, Michael also remarked:

> If you just sit and listen to all the different cells, you will hear a thousand arguments all day, every day, about nothing. It's the anger and frustration everybody feels inside themselves. You have this rage that builds and builds and builds and builds, and little things just make you go crazy.
>
> For instance, mail is the highlight of the day. When you see the officer go past your door, and if you ain't got no mail coming through that door, that can really put a damper on your day. And if you didn't have a piece of bread on your tray, you're supposed to get two pieces of bread on your tray. If I was missing a piece of bread on my tray, I would explode. 'Where's my other piece of bread?' If I didn't have salt on my tray, 'give me my salt. I want my salt now.
>
> If we don't get what we deserve or what we're supposed to have, even if we speak up and snap out and go crazy because we're not getting what we're supposed to have according to their guidelines, we're deemed disruptive to

the security. All these different things stack up on you. We have rules stacked six feet above our heads. Walking in circles and lying down all day makes you want to rebel.

We walk around the cell for hours. You could just walk in circles and circles and circles and circles for hours. I don't expect the administration to understand what we go through behind their doors. In that cell, you just have so much anger. That's how we end up fighting. You got to come into this cell, and you've got to beat me up. You got to beat me up. I want to fight you now. I just have so much pain built up inside of me. I want to just feel it; you know what I'm saying? Give it to me. Don't play with me. Just give it to me all the way.

Long-term solitary confinement is cruel.

§

My heart aches whenever I think that Justin, Josue, Michael, and tens of thousands of people in the U.S. have or are experiencing alienation and abject loneliness for years. When I asked Justin if he felt he would be able to function in society, his response was a resounding and disheartening "No." He had reached the crushing realization that his coping mechanism for dealing with solitude was to harbor negative thoughts about people so as not to desire their companionship. I assumed his days dragged on like a slow-moving river, each hour indistinguishable from the last.

The alarmingly high suicide rates among prisoners subjected to a dismal solitary existence for long periods tragically highlight its destructive power. The stories are not simply tales of suffering. They are a call to action, urging us to address the deep-seated issues that lead to incarceration and the overuse of solitary confinement. We must invest in programs that support individuals in overcoming trauma, improving mental health, and developing life skills. Implementing reforms can create a more compassionate and equitable system prioritizing rehabilitation over punishment, allowing individuals to contribute meaningfully to society. This shift is not just a nice idea but a moral imperative and the key to establishing a humane system of justice.

Our nation is filled with creative individuals capable of generating solutions and opportunities for nearly every social problem. The vital missing elements are adequate funding and a genuine commitment to assisting those we consider unworthy.

NADIR

nadir / 'nā-dər noun. the lowest point, the point
of greatest adversity or despair.

Dictionary.com

In early 2000, I stumbled upon Nadir's profile on a pen
pal site. He stood out in his carefully posed photograph—
pinkish-red, crisp, ironed shirt, head tilted just so, like an
Olan Mills portrait. He described himself as a conscious
African American Muslim of Dominican descent. I thought
he was handsome. Thirty-seven years old, nearing the end of
his sentence, he confessed to having no real plans for the
future. He explained that he sold drugs as a single father,
but then his five-year-old daughter was murdered. nadir
described in graphic detail that he shot her killer upon seeing

the man hanging out in the projects. He approached the dude, said his daughter's name, and popped him.

"That muh'fucka in a wheelchair now. If I ever see him again, I'mma kill him," he wrote, maintaining that he'd never been caught for the shooting.

§

For two years, I wrote to nadir and shared intimate details of my life. I never sent him any money, but I paid for a ton of collect calls. Twice, I traveled from California to New Jersey to visit him. He was shy. Unlike his Olan Mills-esque photo, in which he sported long dreadlocks, his wavy hair was thinning and balding. His face twitched as he spoke, and his words were interrupted involuntarily due to his severe stutter.

During a visit, I questioned an officer about him, even though I knew she was forbidden to discuss prisoners' personal affairs. That was 2001, and the internet was not as generous as it is now. I wasn't surprised that she replied, "I can't talk to you about inmates." Thus, I urged myself to go with the flow and get to know him. I didn't have suspicions about him when I asked, just that I was being nosey.

He often talked about wanting another child since losing his daughter. My raging hormones made me think he could be a prospect. I wanted a baby so bad in my lower 30s that I took prenatal vitamins and bought onesies that I kept in a storage bin. I wasn't even sleeping with anyone.

My journal overflowed with thoughts and reflections on nadir as his release date grew closer, usually concentrated on the fact that he called too damn much—sometimes five or six times per day. Though his calls were filled with sweet words, they came as early as six in the morning, sometimes immediately after we ended a conversation and occasionally just moments after I explicitly demanded space.

"But I miss you," he would say while I rolled my eyes and held the receiver 10 inches from my face.

As the days ticked by, he became more persistent about wanting to live with me in California immediately after his scheduled release from a prison in New Jersey. I had never lived with a partner, and I did not want my first time to be with a man I didn't really know who was coming straight out of prison. Visiting for a week would be cool, but I did not want to make decisions about him staying with me long-term. I did, however, buy him clothes, shoes, and personal items so he could be set upon his release.

When he was released on January 5, 2002, I was a nervous wreck. I had flown to Baltimore for Christmas and stayed for his big day. My stomach churned as I waited for him at the Greyhound station downtown. He stepped off the bus wearing a gray sweatshirt, no-name sneakers, and a jacket too thin for the Baltimore winter. He looked nervous but handsome.

We flew to California the next morning with plans for him to visit for 5 ½ days. He was nervous about socializing and looked to me to speak for him. He did not trust my neighbors at the clubhouse, where we had breakfast once. The elderly White women who gathered there attempted to make small talk with him, and he said he was uncomfortable talking to people he did not know. I chalked this up to social anxiety, typical for people newly released from prison.

We flew to California the next morning for what was supposed to be a 5 ½-day visit. I had bought him new clothes and undergarments, hoping to help him feel more comfortable. But his behavior set off alarm bells almost immediately. He didn't bathe unless I nagged him. He wore

119

the same shirt, pants, and underwear for days, ignoring the fresh outfits I'd laid out for him. His table manners were atrocious. He sought my permission for everything—using the bathroom, stepping outside—as if he couldn't function independently. I chalked it up to post-incarceration anxiety, but I was disappointed.

Everything went to shit on our fourth day together. I invited him to go to the grocery store with me. He declined. This would be the first time he had been alone in my home. I returned but had to knock on the front door because he had secured the top lock, which could only be operated from inside.

A surge of alarm coursed through me when he answered the door wearing the white Reebok sneakers I had purchased for him. My space had always been a shoe-free sanctuary, and I was appalled by his sudden disregard for this rule. His pacing intensified. He claimed that I had received a call from a mysterious man. Strangely, he couldn't recall the man's name. My curiosity quickly turned to concern. He was fidgety. I checked the caller ID, only to find no record of any such call. Waves of nervousness washed over me, and I immediately phoned my friend Rachquel, pleading for her to come over.

Thirty minutes after questioning why a strange man called me, nadir magically remembered his name.

"Ibrahim. Yeah, I remember now."

Immediately, I knew. Ibrahim is a beautiful brother in Baltimore whom I have adored for years. nadir knew his name because he rummaged through my file cabinet and found my diary, a trove of secrets spanning more than five years. Every admission of shame, vulnerability, and fear was scribbled in that two-toned blue book, and a chunk of it was about his poor hygiene, his submissive disposition, and my sense that we would not survive as a couple. I jetted to the closet. My eyes were fixated on the empty pillowcase that used to hold my diary. Now, the case was wrinkled and stuffed under a small box. I stood motionless, more stunned than the warden in The Shawshank Redemption discovering a big ass hole in the wall.

nadir scurried to the bathroom and locked himself in. I bolted to the hallway and began pounding. "Give me my fucking diary!" In that instant, a whirlwind of emotions flooded me—rage coursed through my veins, betrayal seared my heart, and a primal need to safeguard the words meant only for my god and me.

At first, he was silent. Then he responded with a lie. "I don't know what you're talking about." He had not thought this through. Locked in my bathroom with nowhere else to go, he was stuck.

"Give me my goddamn diary, or I am calling the police." My hands shook as I pounded on the door, and my breath came in shallow gasps. I hammered the door with the bottom of my foot for another minute and then darted to the kitchen to dial the police.

The phone rang. I held it to my ear and waited, my heart thumping in my chest. Finally, a dispatcher's voice cracked through the line. "9-1-1, what's your emergency?"

I took a deep breath and began to speak. "I have a man in my house who was released from prison a few days ago, and I want him out of here." I said it loud enough for him to hear me.

He peeked out from the bathroom into the kitchen. "I can't believe you called the pigs, Nandi. That's fucked up." His words stuttered as his eyes blinked.

"Get out!" I exclaimed. "Gimme my shit and get out." I clenched my teeth and spoke with a low roar. He left my apartment, still insisting he knew nothing about a diary.

Moments later, a young officer arrived, saying nadir had just caught him outside and wanted me to know that the diary was stuffed in the cushions of my couch. He told nadir to stay away, and that was supposed to be that.

Rachquel showed up while he was wandering around outside. She was aware of all I had done for him—the countless hours of kindness and support, the cross-country trips, and the endless hours of phone conversations. I told Rachquel he deserved to read the ugly things I wrote about him, and it served his ass right. Still, I was embarrassed by other things he might have read.

Rachquel assured me that my heart was in the right place. I questioned my judgment and how I could have allowed myself to be tangled up with him. His incessant calls to me clearly showed he didn't respect boundaries. Rachquel rubbed my back as I coddled my forehead in my hands. The winter evening was in full swing, with the sky already dark and the temperature dropping. After two to three hours, she left and promised she'd call to check on me later. My shoulders softened, and my breathing slowed. I wished she wouldn't leave me, but she had a kid and a husband waiting.

My two-year investment culminated in three days of subpar intimacy with a man whose meager social skills and poor hygiene led me to pound on my bathroom door while he hid pitifully on the other side. I was equally angry with myself as I was with him. How could I have been so naïve? I should have known something was wrong when he catfished me with that Olan Mills-y picture.

The night was marked by a relentless barrage of phone

calls from the payphone at 7-11, one block away. I hung up on him repeatedly. At one point, I answered, cursed at him until my lips quivered, and then hung up again. He seemed fine with me cursing as long as he had access to me.

It was January and cold. Before she left, Rachquel convinced me to let nadir sleep in my car until the following day. I set a suitcase full of his clothes on the porch and clicked the unlock button on my key fob from my upstairs apartment. I arranged a trip for him back to New Jersey, wrote his flight information on a post-it note, and stuck it on the suitcase. The following morning, a taxi came for him, and that was the last time I saw nadir, marking the start of unforeseen twists and turns.

He returned to the east coast and crashed on his mom's couch for a few months. He called me back-to-back for weeks, sometimes dozens of times every day, begging for a second chance. He inundated my answering machine with desperate messages. Each message was a psychotic blend of apologies and insults. One night, he left nineteen messages.

"Fat bitch." Click.

"I love you so much, Nandi. Please call me back." Click.

"I can't believe I thought you were wifey material. Whore." Click.

"I'm sorry. Nandi, pick up the phone. Hello?" Click.

"I need you. Call me back, please." Click.

"I don't need you, bitch." Click.

Back then, calls were either local or long-distance. AT&T contacted me and asked if I had authorized more than 300 long-distance calls on my calling card. No, the fuck I did not. The card had been in the glove compartment of my car before he got in. Lo and goddamn behold, he was not just a pain in my ass; he was a thief. In addition to stealing my card, he took my CD case, a few unpaid bills, and an inexpensive necklace, none of which I realized were gone. I changed my number and refused all the mail he sent. Fortunately, I was off the hook with AT&T for all the calls.

Approximately six months after he left, I received a call from a woman named Denise, an old girlfriend of his. She stumbled upon my number on her phone bill, as several of his late-night rants were made from her home. She confronted him, and he told her made-up stories about a luxurious life he and I lived together. Denise and I spoke daily for weeks, comparing examples of his unhinged behavior. She shared that there were days when she rounded the corner of her apartment to find him crouched in the bushes under her window. She was terrified of him, and we agreed he was sick. Listening to Denise recount her experiences, I felt a mix of shock, horror, and a deep sense of relief that I had sent his ass packing.

But his calls kept coming. In one message, he rejoiced that he had found his daughter. Huh? The one who was murdered? Yeah, her. It was as if he had forgotten or did not care that he told me he shot and paralyzed the man responsible for her death. Later, he left a voicemail saying he had returned to California, living an hour from me. He said he knew my new address. The thought of him brazenly showing up at my home angered me more than it frightened me. Allowing him into my life in the first place had been a source of profound embarrassment. His audacity knew no bounds. He went as far as contacting the university's president, smearing my reputation by falsely accusing me of stalking his fictitious son, whom he claimed was a student.

I immediately filed a report with the campus police. Within days, a cop called and said I should report to his office as soon as I could. I rushed across campus and rushed inside the trailer that acted as the temporary police department. After a few "ums" and "ahs," he shared that nadir had recently been released from prison. I already knew that. What I did not know was that he had just served twelve years for the brutal rape of a girl under the age of 14. The officer then shared that he had a dozen aliases and numerous social security numbers to conceal prior offenses. nadir was an extremely dangerous and unpredictable person.

I am only slightly exaggerating when I say my face cracked and fell to the floor. Ha' mercy, Jesus! I could not sleep for days. I eventually found him on the sex offender registry, and his shameful face was listed under Rajah Ukawabutu.

§

Over the next year, he bombarded me with phone calls and hang-ups at work. Late-night rants flooded my office voicemail, filled with insults and name-calling. Like a broken record, nadir would follow up one nasty message after another with a hollow and insincere apology. It was painfully evident that he had not changed. Despite my attempts to ignore him and move on, the calls persisted, relentlessly draining me emotionally and mentally.

Then, one day, the calls stopped. The eerie silence brought me relief but was cause for suspicion. I couldn't shake the feeling that this might be a temporary respite, a deceptive lull before the storm. Just when I thought the storm had retreated, a letter arrived at my office. It was written from jail, claiming he had been wrongfully imprisoned. This time, he vehemently claimed that it was a matter of self-defense. In the letter, he said he wanted me to speak at his funeral if anything happened to him because I was his only real friend. His plea struck me as a painfully transparent reflection of his deep-seated desperation.

§

Five years after leaving my home and violating his required quarterly check-in with the sex offender registry service, nadir committed another assault. According to an online news report, he broke into a woman's house in Whitesboro, New Jersey, entering through an open window in her attic. He held metal against her body and raped her. He pleaded guilty once confronted with DNA evidence. The Superior Court judge, as noted in the online news story, said nadir had been arrested 22 times in the last 25 years, which was especially egregious given that he had spent twelve of those years incarcerated.

Psychiatrists who evaluated him for the Whitesboro trial delivered a chilling diagnosis: an antisocial personality fueled by a dangerous blend of hostile and sexual impulses and a hedonistic obsession with sexual activity. The judge handed down a sentence of twenty years for the rape.

In July 2023, he was housed at the New Jersey Adult Diagnostic Treatment Center (ADTC). According to the National Institute of Justice, ADTC is a "facility that provides cognitive-behavioral treatment services aimed at reducing the recidivism rates of adult sex offenders. The program targets repetitive, compulsive sex offenders in the New Jersey correctional system who are receptive to receiving treatment. Cognitive-behavioral treatments focus on reconstructing offenders' cognitive distortions; relapse prevention focuses on pattern recognition and breaking the cycle of recommitting sex crimes." I really, really, really, really, really hope the program worked for him. I signed up to receive notifications of his release, and an alert pinged my phone on October 18, 2023, announcing his release. The fact that he served 20 years to the day lets me know that they kept him as long as he could, and he was not given even a one-day reprieve for good behavior, parole, or probation.

He had better not contact me. Bastard.

SEX OFFENDER HELL

Honesty is more than not lying. It is truth telling, truth speaking, truth living, and truth
loving.

James E. Faust

I was apprehensive when Saul showed up at my house.
He was a sex offender whom I had met on the internet. I
looked through the peephole and wondered if allowing him
to come to my house was a good idea. For those few seconds,
I stood motionless on the interior side of my door, reflecting
on the nadir fiasco.

Saul found me online in the spring of 2011 when he
noticed my prisoner advocacy work. He invited me to view
his blog, which detailed his struggles with being on the sex-

offender registry. He felt like a victim of society's judgment, unable to break through the preconceived notions people hold about sex offenders. We chatted for a couple of months through his blog, focusing mainly on the pros and cons of the registry. Our conversations were friendly.

He inspired me to ask questions about the validity of the registry in my women's studies and gender studies courses.

"Perhaps one day, you can be a guest speaker in my class and make your case to my students." I did not know he would take me seriously.

Months later, Saul asked if he could stop by my house during a road trip from Washington State to visit family in southern California. "Sure," I said, imagining he would spend a few hours and move along. Then I invited him to campus to speak to my classes. Saul jumped at the opportunity. Grateful for a captive audience, he hit the road.

The national sex offender registry provides a means for community members to know about potential risks in their area. It also helps law enforcement track sex offenders to ensure they comply with the conditions of their release. Believing that being on the registry made it difficult for individuals to find housing or employment, Saul felt discriminated against and advocated for eradicating the registry. He felt like a victim and a target of harassment, judgment, and alienation.

§

Saul's father performed lewd sexual acts on him and his sister when they were children. His dad told them that he was "teaching them about pleasure" as he molested them. That warped foundation set Saul on a path of blurred lines and bad decisions. His father was a Hollywood bigwig who won numerous awards for his work behind the camera, and he eventually shot and killed himself.

Unlike nadir, Saul was open to sharing the stories behind his crimes. Mostly, though, he wanted to focus on the discrimination that those on the registry faced. I was interested in understanding the politics of the registry, and I could support the cause as long as it aligned with my understanding.

I was confident that the students in my Sociology of Gender class, my Introduction to Women's Studies course, and the two sections of Introduction to Sociology would be eager to interact with him, but I was uncertain if they would remain receptive once they discovered his past actions. At 27 years old and addicted to alcohol and drugs, he committed his first crime and went to jail in the early 1990s.

While in a drunken stupor, he walked into his housemate's bedroom, hoping to rouse her out of her sleep. He kissed her between her thighs, and she awoke petrified. Yanked from the pages of campy pornography, Saul had hoped she would awaken aroused and want to engage in sex. As he explained, her bewilderment jolted him out of his intoxicated state, so he apologized and dashed from her room.

While he claimed to accept full responsibility for the offense, he did not understand why she was still so angry as to not want to ever converse with him given that so many years had passed. The events of that night sparked a tumultuous, decades-long journey of arrests, rehab, lawsuits, drug use, failed relationships, and an online chat that led him to my front door.

After serving a year in the Los Angeles County Jail, charged with attempted oral copulation/sexual battery on his housemate years before Megan's Law, Saul was free to move on without the public knowing what he had done. He left California to pursue an intimate partnership in Colorado, where he began working as an apartment manager. After peering through her window for weeks and watching her walk half-clothed around her apartment, he then made the same egregious choice to enter a woman's space without her consent.

He used the master key to enter her apartment while she slept. He said he had not reached her bed before she awoke and screamed. Just as he had been six years prior, he was thrust into sobriety, apologized, lied about his reason for being there, and departed. He was again arrested and charged with a sex crime, but not before the woman's guy friend came over and kicked Saul's ass.

In response to this second offense, a judge offered him a choice: a short jail stint or two years of sex offender therapy. Saul chose therapy but resented every moment of it. He rejected the program's framework, which he felt painted him as a monster instead of a man struggling with addiction. When he failed to register his address after moving to Washington, the law caught up with him again. He gained little from the program and filed a court order to leave. Saddled with the Colorado charge, Saul was placed on the national sex offender registry.

In our conversations, he expressed little awareness of the impact he had on those women, and his expressions of contrition seemed to suggest he was tired of saying, "I'm sorry." Not knowing him, I was unsure whether he genuinely understood how his choices would impact the women for the remainder of their lives. His focus was mainly on getting to the parts of the story he was most passionate about, namely, saying the registry and his father are the problems. One of his criticisms was that there was no narrative connected to someone's name, just codes, and tiers that are supposed to indicate one's likelihood to re-offend. He was certain he would not do those things again.

He eventually moved back to the west coast but failed to follow a court order to update his address on the registry within 30 days. One night, while he was driving drunk with a busted taillight, a police officer pulled him over. Learning that he was a sex offender, the police officer wanted to know how long Saul had been in Washington. Because it had been more than 30 days, he was hauled off to jail again on a failure-to-report charge.

§

When Saul addressed my classes, he laid out the facts of his life. He described his struggles with addiction, the registry's limitations, and his encounters with law enforcement. He painted himself as a man trying to reform but repeatedly beaten down by a system that wouldn't let him move on.

But he was careful with his words. He left out key details in some stories, like how he had watched his second victim for weeks before entering her apartment. He omitted the fact that he didn't register his address because he thought he could get away with it. He focused on being targeted by the police and hung up on the stigma of being labeled a Level 3 offender—the "worst of the worst."

I had heard him tell the story of his criminality from start to finish six times: once before we met in person, once before we drove to campus, and four times during the day while he spoke to my students. Usually, his story was linear and contained all the essential elements, but he sometimes left out significant parts, depending on the reception he received from the class.

For example, in his first iteration of the story, he told me he watched the second victim through a window for weeks before he entered her apartment with his master key. He never mentioned that to my students because the reception was colder than he had hoped.

Other times, he left out the fact that he did not register when he moved to Washington, just that a cop harassed him and carted him off to jail. He stated that his photo was hung in the local post office as proof that he was being targeted and mistreated. When speaking in my women's studies class, he said he did not register because he had not yet secured an address to report to the authorities. When he and I talked on the way to campus, I asked if he had committed violations against women that did not become criminal offenses. He admitted he had. That fact never came out when he stood at the front of my classrooms because it was out of alignment with his desire to be viewed as a victim.

Despite knowing that we all do impression management work, I saw Saul as disingenuous and manipulative, not simply because he attempted to manage our impression of him but because my biases about sex crimes made his behavior personal. Perhaps my experiences as a woman who experienced men with horrid boundaries and passive-aggressive approaches to sex made me less sympathetic. Even with my social justice leanings, I struggled.

§

My last class ended at 9 p.m., and he asked if he could sleep at my place before getting on the road. I told him that would be fine, but I was wary. When we arrived back at my house, I was all talked out, and frankly, I was ready for him to leave. I also did not want him to get to know me any more than what we shared online or throughout the day.

After I showed him the guest room, I told him I would see him in the morning. I went to my bedroom—and locked the door behind me.

Around midnight, I heard the sound of my doorknob rattling. My heart seized. I froze, gripping the edge of my blanket. "Nandi?" Saul's voice came softly through the door.

"What do you want?" I called out, forcing my voice to remain calm.

"Do you have a towel I can use?" he asked.

I stayed still for a moment, assessing the situation. "Give me a second," I finally replied. I flicked on the light and cracked open the door. "Next time, knock," I said, handing him a towel.

My fight instinct kicked in, and I had a bit of bass in my voice.

"Oh, sorry." He was passive and aggressive.

My tone was a holdover from feelings I developed throughout the day.

That night, I struggled to reconcile my feelings. I wanted to believe in Saul's potential for redemption, but I couldn't ignore the patterns in his behavior. He claimed to be misunderstood, yet he offered no real acknowledgment of the harm he had caused. He spoke passionately about the injustice of the registry but dismissed his victims' pain.

I looked up Saul's name online in 2024 and found that he owns a compound that hosts getaways and personal wellness retreats out in the middle of nature. Immediately, I thought about the possibility that he peeps at women through the windows of his cabins, and I wondered if those women know who he is.

My work as a sociologist has taught me that trauma

often perpetuates cycles of harm. But I've also learned that redemption requires accountability and growth. Saul, it seemed, wanted the former without the latter.

I have not given much thought to the sex offender registry since Saul left, but I have questioned its purpose. Does it protect the public, or does it shame people into hiding? Does it offer a path to rehabilitation, or does it simply create more barriers? For now, I remain unsure. But when it comes to Saul, I am certain of one thing: he has massive issues with boundaries and accountability. And no registry can fix that.

THE WEIGHT OF SECOND CHANCES

Even love unreturned has its rainbow.

J.M. Barrie

I told Joe I would not write about him in my book. During our last conversation, he defiantly declared, "Go 'head and write that chapter," and then hung up. Writing is an emotional outlet for me, and finding words to help me understand our full story feels like work I need to do. So, here goes—a tiny piece of the adventure that is my connection to Joe.

Over the years, our relationship has been a savory blend of intensity, joy, support, and frustration—often intertwined simultaneously. Due to our current estrangement, I'll focus this chapter mostly on one of our better experiences; I have already hurt Joe enough.

Our paths first crossed early in 2010 when I toured California State Prison Sacramento, also known as New Folsom, in preparation for the "Prison Industrial Complex" class I was teaching. I intended to have my students visit the facility the following semester, so I wanted to experience it myself first. During the tour, which lasted around two hours, a lieutenant accompanied me through the housing units, administrative areas, the main yard, classrooms, and the law library, where Joe worked as a clerk. Curious about the racial dynamics of the prison population, I probed the lieutenant for insights, and he suggested I direct my questions to Joe.

Joe is ten years younger than I am. He was a 29-year-old White guy with thick glasses and a warm smile framed by a reddish-brown beard. I did not yet know that he was serving two life sentences without the possibility of parole, but it did not matter. He was a nice guy.

I asked Joe to teach me about race relations in the prison, and he responded honestly and thoughtfully. He concluded that his placement on a sensitive needs yard, rather than the mainline, made a big difference in the level of racial tension. We engaged in an unsupervised conversation for nearly 20 minutes, with me leaning against the checkout counter and Joe standing at the edge while the lieutenant conversed outside the library. As our time together concluded, I expressed gratitude and a desire to continue our discussion at some point.

Following the tour, I asked the lieutenant if it would be okay for me to correspond with Joe, to which he replied, "I'll ask him." In a subsequent email, I thanked the lieutenant for the tour, reassured him that my students and I would see him the following semester, and reminded him that I wanted permission to write to Joe. He replied with Joe's mailing address.

Before my students and I showed up to New Folsom in the fall, Joe had been transferred to another facility in central California. It was far away—five hours by car. We wrote to each other a lot, and it did not take long before we allowed ourselves to become vulnerable.

In a letter from 2011, he said he had been coping with shame and feeling down. He wrote the following:

> I have learned his name and spoken it. By do-
> ing so, I have brought the full burden of his
> assault upon my being to bear the punishment
> I have inflicted upon myself. It is called guilt.
> It brands me with a shame so deep and pene-
> trating that I have been reduced to a mere
> shadow of the man I could have been. So vi-
> cious is this beating that I am unable to raise
> my head in defiance. For when I do, when I
> look into the eyes of this monster pummeling
> me incessantly, I see the once-innocent boy I
> was—with all his potential for greatness—
> wearing anger I no longer feel.

In response, I wrote, "If you can begin to see yourself as I see you—as a deep, profoundly reflective, complex, warm, beautiful person—then perhaps you will agree with me that you are worthy of compassion, of being cared for, of having a second chance."

I hadn't yet visited him when I wrote that, nor had he had any visits from anyone in a decade. Soon, I began traveling to central California to see him, sometimes multiple times per month. During our visits, we shared details of our lives. We genuinely liked each other. As we sat together in the visiting room or on the patio, he would sometimes stare at me with a gaze filled with affection. He often complimented my appearance. His pale skin burned quickly or was already peeling from his days out in the direct sun days before. He was bald, and I would insist that he use the sunscreen I purchased for him a few times in the quarterly packages of pastries, shoes, underwear, headphones, digital music, and lots of Folgers coffee.

Despite the limited time, we developed a deep connection and understanding of each other. It felt like we were making the most of a difficult situation, finding happiness and hope amid hardship. Our visits were sometimes challenging. He'd smile and tell me to stay strong, and I'd reassure him that he was worthy of being loved. In those moments, our bond was solidified, surpassing the confines of the prison walls. We were kindred spirits, brought together by circumstance yet connected by a profound understanding of the human condition.

As our visits went on and we spoke daily on the phone, our conversations began to take a more serious turn. He opened up about his childhood and the choices that led him to prison. He was shared his deepest fears and regrets. In turn, I shared my own struggles and insecurities. We sought solace in each other's stories, finding comfort in our experiences. We may have come from very different backgrounds, but we had both faced hardship and pain.

Our connection was rooted in our mutual need to feel seen and heard. The more we talked, the more we realized how much we had in common. We had both experienced loss and heartbreak. We had both faced difficult choices, and we had both made mistakes. But we were committed to doing better and finding a way forward. Through our conversations, we found hope. Once or twice, I was not honest with him about who I was "messing around with." I'll save those stories for my diary.

Our conversations included what we hoped to achieve. Joe spoke of wanting to help young people. I shared my desire to use my experiences to help others, too, and to share my sociological knowledge to make an impact on the world. We both wanted to give back and find a way to turn our pain into something positive. We expressed an abundance of laughter and tears and found comfort in each other that we hadn't experienced before. We became so close that he was the only person I mentioned on the dedication page of my last book. His presence in my life during that time was a powerful force for good, and our connection left me feeling loved, supported, and empowered. While I was able to help him in some ways, I hoped I had the most significant impact on helping him see his own worth; he deserved forgiveness, love, and compassion.

What was most remarkable about Joe, though, was not his intelligence or his vast stores of knowledge. It was his humility. He earned multiple college degrees; on the last count, he had completed enough college credits to earn five associate's degrees, one after another, with no interest in applying for graduation or collecting diplomas. He merely craved learning. He also handwrote his autobiography and two academic-quality articles he shared with me. Joe is immodest and even mildly egotistical about his smarts, but he is humble and often even self-deprecating.

Joe is also a talented artist, and I am lucky to own

several of his original acrylic and charcoal paintings, including portraits of Dr. Angela Davis and Bob Marley. He had heard he could earn money selling his art. I created an auction on my Facebook page, and one of my former students purchased his Bob Marley piece for $99 but never picked it up. I also hosted his work on eBay but kept it for myself since it did not sell.

Regrettably, Joe was burdened with the weight of restitution and faced a steep 55% fee on every dollar he received by mail. We devised several clever solutions to help him acquire commissary items. First, I began purchasing greeting cards from Dollar Tree, which Joe could then sell to fellow inmates. The cards, priced at two for $1, allowed him to make a profit and improve his financial situation. Another way I assisted was by printing captivating photos from the internet at Walgreens for just 23¢ each. These images became highly sought-after among the prisoners, featuring tattoo symbols, motorcycles, and impressive Aztec statues. Joe successfully traded these printed photos for commissary goods like coffee, stamps, art supplies, and hygiene items. Each transaction became a lifeline, granting him access to items that brought relief, diversion, and a brief respite from the prison menu.

§

I began making friends with women who visited their partners. Pauletta was a sister from Los Angeles who I trusted, even though Joe said her man, Bam, was shady as fuck. To save money, Pauletta and I shared a motel room two times, a decision that gave me a sense of comfort and familiarity. However, in my comfort, I made a grave misstep—I divulged the details behind Joe's third life sentence to Pauletta, oblivious that most other prisoners did not know. Pauletta told Bam, and Joe was hurt that I shared his business. He is now open about the fact that he killed his cellmate in a fistfight one night when they were both drunk.

In preparation for my publication of *This Side of My Struggle*, Joe distributed my call for submissions around the prison. My name and university address were on the flyer. Bam, Pauletta's shady dude, used that information to write to me at the university, saying he'd been watching me in the visiting room. His letter was uncouth and entirely out of pocket. I immediately contacted Pauletta to tell her, but she did not believe me. When Joe called me later in the evening, I read Bam's letter to him. He sounded calm but assured me he would take care of it. The next time Joe and Bam were outside on the yard, Joe approached Bam and busted him square in the mouth. When I asked him what he'd done, he initially hesitated to tell me but assured me I wouldn't receive any more mail from Bam.

The next time I saw Pauletta was in the visiting room. She entered to see Bam seated with another woman. Pauletta caused a massive scene. Bam repeatedly told her to sit down, but she screamed obscenities even as the officers escorted her out amid a sea of shocked faces. She returned an hour later and sat calmly with Bam and the other woman.

§

I also saw Mia in the visiting room one day while waiting for Joe to enter. I had briefly corresponded with her after finding her on a prison pen pal site, around the same time I met Joe. Mia is a transgender woman initially sentenced to death for murder. Although I despise every aspect of her crime, I am against the death penalty and was impressed that she fought on her own behalf to have the conviction overturned. When I saw her in the visiting room, I immediately recognized her from the pen pal photo. She had a towering build, a bald head, and striking blue eyeshadow. However, the correctional officer prohibited us from officially introducing ourselves because it is strictly forbidden to interact with anyone other than the inmate you were visiting.

Mia had been fighting for the fair treatment of trans prisoners for years, once protesting the ban on bras in men's prisons for those like herself who had breast implants; she ran across the open yard with her bare breasts exposed. Her display of resistance helped change the policy surrounding transgender prisoners throughout the state. I told Joe about Mia and asked him to introduce himself to her. He did and became one of the few prisoners who treated her kindly.

§

Joe is capable of deep empathy and compassion. I saw the pain he carried, the regret that haunted him. And I saw how sensitive and beautiful he was. When he extended a heartfelt invitation for me to meet his family, I delightedly accepted. It had been more than 13 years since Joe's mom, Veronica, last saw him. In that time, she had given birth to a son named Will. When I entered their lives, Will was an energetic 10-year-old. Joe spoke of his little brother with overwhelming emotion and told me his baby brother was the impetus for getting and staying on the straight and narrow. He is deeply in touch with his emotions anyway, but anything concerning Will gets him choked up.

When I met Joe's family for the first time, I treated them to dinner at their favorite Mexican restaurant. Will was the cutest boy I'd had the pleasure of knowing. He was not the least bit shy. He was bouncy and outgoing, and his jokes were corny, but we laughed, and I was delighted to be around him.

Veronica emanated an air of modesty and resilience, her unassuming presence. With a mild-mannered disposition, she exuded a subdued strength. Despite her Caucasian heritage, her skin boasted an olive tone. Her hair was graying, and her weathered face was a testament to a life of grace and hardship. Her most striking feature was her deep-set eyes.

Grady, her husband, was crude and vulgar. He was a Black man in his 60s who verbally abused everyone, including Veronica and Will. Grady often sat in a wheelchair that he pulled forward with his feet. He had 12 other kids from previous relationships, but Will was the only one in his life. While I'm not sure why Veronica stayed married to him, it's possible she couldn't bear the thought of Will growing up without a father, as Joe had. Or perhaps her loyalty was rooted in the love she once had for him, back when times were better.

On one occasion, while I was visiting Joe's family, we sat on the front porch of their modest home. Grady was seated next to me. Will was perched on two flat pillows on the ground between my legs while I cornrowed his hair. Grady made an offensive comment to me, which I can no longer recall, but his son's response was a quick reach-around slap on his dad's leg.

"Don't say that to her," Will asserted.

Before I could cosign his comment, his father reached over me and slapped Will relatively hard on the shoulder. "Boy, don't you ever fucking put your hands on me. I'll fuck you up. I don't know who you think you are. Hitting me 'cause of some woman you don't even know. I'm your goddamn father," he sneered.

Will looked at the ground, his eyes averted and his

shoulders drooping. I gently nudged his head up and away from his dad as he mumbled an almost inaudible apology. "Sorry."

"Sorry, my ass." His father continued to rant about the leg slap before veering off and mentioning a gun. I was shocked and uneasy. My stomach was in knots, but I said nothing and continued focusing on my fingers in Will's hair. That was not the first time I saw Grady cursing and scowling, but it was the first time I was caught in the crosshairs. He often made demeaning comments to Veronica. She would force a smile, but the tension in her eyes betrayed her. It was a challenging environment.

I loved the bond I formed with Will; he reminded me of my baby brother, who had died six years earlier. In less than a year, I became close enough to Veronica and Will that she asked me to be Will's guardian should anything happen to her. She gave me an official copy of Will's birth certificate and other important information. I was grateful she saw me that way. Veronica and Will had become my family, too, and I called her Mama V sometimes. I'd forgotten that intimate fact until recently when I stumbled across an old email I'd sent her asking if she felt comfortable telling me the story of how she met Joe's dad.

I imagine I was as much a lifeline for her and Joe as she was for me. In a typed letter from later in 2011, I wrote to Joe, "One reason I spend time with your mom is that she keeps me tied to the part of you that was pure, as in childhood-pure. The stories she tells me about you and the animals you nursed, how you talked in your sleep, and your fussy food choices remind me that you had a life before prison.

§

I asked Veronica if I could take Will to the prison to meet Joe. To my delight, her face lit up. She wholeheartedly embraced the idea with an affirming nod and a warm smile. Will jumped up and down and could not wait to meet his big brother. His energy was so infectious that I was swept up in it, too. The night before our trip, Veronica graciously invited me to stay the night in their two-bedroom home with the three of them and the dozens of pets they had. I lived two hours north, and the prison was another three and a half hours south, so I accepted the invitation. She didn't want to join us on the trip.

Before dinner the night before our trip, while Veronica and Will were outside, Grady offered me $50 to lick my vagina. When I told him hell no, he asked if he could smell it. Hell. No. I shared what he said to me with Veronica. She had already witnessed him say inappropriate shit to me, but she still asked him if it was true. He told her I was lying.

Later that night, Joe called, and I informed him what his stepfather had the nerve to say to me. "Put him on the phone."

I handed Grady my phone and watched his face go blank. His eyes danced from me to the floor. When he gave me the phone back, I asked Joe what he said. "I took care of it," was all he told me. Grady did not talk to me for the rest of the evening, which was fine with me.

Will and I hit the road at 3:30 a.m. On the way, we picked up Lupe, also a regular at the prison and a woman I had befriended on multiple visits. She lived just outside of Sacramento and was excellent company during the journey, as Will had a 100% success rate for falling asleep the second a car was in motion.

As the dawn stretched across the horizon, we found

ourselves closer to the prison compound. By the time we reached the area near the prison at 7 o'clock, a muggy haze had begun to blanket the area. We were fifth in line on the side of the road. Visitors were not allowed onto the lot until an hour before check-in, so we parked, waited for an officer to wave the cars in, and then stood in the line leading up to the main building. Once inside, Will and I found our way to a small table in the front near the officer's desk, anxiously awaiting Joe's entrance to the visiting room. Despite the sounds of inmates and their visitors, I focused only on Will.

"Are you nervous, or are you happy?"

"Happy," he replied, bouncing with boundless energy. Will's excitement was overwhelming, and he talked and talked while my nerves danced on edge. Time seemed to stretch infinitely until, finally, Joe stepped into the visiting room, quickening his pace as he approached the officer's desk to show his ID. Will's eyes widened with adoration and awe as he rushed into his brother's arms. The tears that welled up in Joe's eyes mirrored my own. Will could not contain his excitement, and his animated laughter was a spectacle of pure affection. They held each other tightly for a few seconds. I couldn't swallow the lump in my throat. I wished their mom was there to see it.

For the next hour, Will talked a mile a minute while Joe listened intently. It was both beautiful and heartbreaking to witness. I purchased a few tokens so they could take photos, and I enjoyed watching them be goofy with each other as they posed for pictures. Seeing them outside on the patio, Joe carrying Will on his shoulders, playing catch with a Nerf football, chasing each other, and eating all the snacks I bought from the vending machine was touching. It was hard not to be moved by the joy shared between the brothers when they met for the first time. Their bond grew stronger with each passing hour, and it was clear that this visit gave Will a sense of connection he didn't have with his dad.

The officer's voice boomed through the room. "Visiting hours are now over."

Will said, "I don't want to go."

Even though we would be together again the next day, their separation was intense. They embraced again, and Joe lifted Will so his feet dangled. I could see Joe's half-smile was hiding his genuine emotions of sadness. His heart was breaking, too.

As the visiting room emptied and Joe was the last to leave, I told Will we had to go. They stared at each other as they walked in opposite directions until Will and I could no longer see Joe. Once in the parking lot, Will could not stop talking about how much fun he had with his big brother and excitedly looked forward to visiting him again the next day. The emotional toll of the day hit me hard. The entire experience was tinged with exhaustion, and I felt raw. Fatigue from the long drive and the lack of sleep caused my patience to be thin, and Will's energy seemed to increase even more than it had when he and his brother giggled and tumbled in the grass on the patio—and talked and talked and talked.

§

Lupe reconnected with us outside near the car. We then checked into the only motel in town before finding somewhere to eat. Lupe rented a room next to ours, and I hung out with her in her room. Will stayed in the room he shared with me and watched TV until he fell asleep.

§

While riding down the highway toward the prison the following morning, I noticed a cotton field off to the left. I had driven past this field numerous times but did not notice or even know cotton grew in California. The sea of white that stretched as far as the eye could see was a visceral reminder of the brutal exploitation and dehumanization of enslaved Black people who were forced to pick cotton from can't-see-in-the-morning-til-can't-see-at-night in the sweltering heat, often with little food or water. I pulled over and asked Lupe to snap a photo of me tugging on one piece with the fingers of my right hand inches away from the word "freedom" tattooed on the inside of my right arm. The contrast was intense.

After the photo, we continued the rest of the way down to join the cars on the side of the road waiting to enter the prison grounds. Once we made it into the parking lot, we finally entered the check-in area after standing in line for over 40 minutes with an overly enthusiastic 10-year-old on a sweltering summer morning. The officer said my shirt was not long enough to cover my skirt and that I needed a longer skirt or pants. Unfortunately, I had only brought that skirt, which I had worn the day before, and some jeans for the drive. Visitors cannot wear blue jeans inside California prisons because the inmates' uniforms are blue denim.

I needed a backup plan, and I needed it fast. I darted back to the car, with Will yelling from the lobby entrance for me to hurry up. Desperately rummaging through his suitcase in the trunk of my car, I searched for one of his shirts to tie around my waist or any shorts he might have had that I could throw under my skirt. He was eager to see his brother and kept yelling for me, "Come on!" Ultimately, I resorted to wearing the same shirt I had worn the previous day. We

The Weight of Second Chances

made it inside and had another beautiful visit with Joe.

§

After the long drive north, I dropped off Lupe outside of Sacramento. Exhausted and emotionally spent, I took Will home and drove a couple of hours back to my house.

In her next call from Joe, Veronica expressed to him she was upset that I had not given her a heads-up about Lupe riding along. She added that she resented that I had her son around someone who trafficked drugs into the prison. I had no idea where that came from. She also wanted to know why Will's clothes had been tossed around in his suitcase. I was distraught when Joe told me what his mother had said. It felt like she was pushing me away, perhaps in response to what I shared about Grady's nasty comments. When he conveyed all this to me, I begged him to reassure her that I would never expose her son or myself to anyone trafficking drugs, and the clothes in his suitcase were only a mess because I was looking for something to wear in a hurry.

Alas, Grady said I was no longer welcome in their home, so I never saw them again. Will and Veronica moved to the Midwest two years later when Grady died.

§

Although I loved Joe, I needed something else— something more. The echo of laughter with his brother and the spirited discussions with his mom were gone. I told him he, his mom, and his brother were a package deal. I was tongue-tied and tormented when he challenged me on that. I still cared for him, but staying connected to Joe felt like work, and I was tired. My shifting emotions left him shattered, so my words fell flat. I soon stopped writing and opening his letters.

After not speaking for a couple of years, I reached out to him in 2015. Our dynamic was different. He seemed afraid to get close again. Hearing him say "Lu you" instead of "I love you" at the end of our phone calls showed me he was afraid to get close again. We maintained a strong enough connection for me to ask him to write the foreword to this book, though. The manuscript was not fully developed then, but I saved his beautiful narrative and included it at the opening of this edition.

Soon, we stopped speaking again. I began dating a transgender man. Joe became upset. For the next couple of years, he referred to my now ex-partner as "that so-called trans guy you were seeing." He isn't transphobic. I think he didn't believe me.

A couple more years passed before he called or wrote again, and I shared with him that I had married someone in prison who was not keen on me maintaining connections with prisoners. I knew the news would devastate him. Indeed, I heard the disappointment in his voice. I thought I had made the right decision about the person I was with, and I didn't want to justify my actions or feel guilty about them. Still, I knew he was hurt.

It had been a couple of years since our last conversation and our last disagreement that left us distant. In the spring of 2022, I composed a letter expressing my continued love for him while acknowledging that the unpredictability of our conflicts had taken a toll and that I couldn't handle another conflict. Guilt and regret weighed heavily on me because he was so nice. I also conveyed my opinion that his lack of opportunity to mature was one of the fundamental issues that drew me away from him. Now 43 years old in 2023, he has been imprisoned for 25 years.

In his reply, he accused me of being present only when I was single. Although I beg to differ, I understand why he felt that way. If there was any truth to his accusation, it is because I am too pained to express any part of my day-to-day life with him that involves loving someone else.

§

From the beginning of our journey together, Joe emphasized the vital importance of transparency. With utmost sincerity, he shared the chilling details of the crimes that had led to his life without parole sentence. In his unwavering quest to provide me with a comprehensive understanding, he mailed me his legal papers unsolicited so that I could examine the case for myself.

Although I cannot recall if the documents specifically labeled him as a shooter, he assured me that he had not shot anyone, just that he was charged because everyone involved was convicted. Joe had made terrible choices, having only turned 18 in December, a mere month before the crimes.

In the first incident, he sat in the front seat of a vehicle while another individual parked the car, walked into a house, and killed a man named Kevin the husband of Lisa. Kevin was brutally murdered in his bed with three gunshots to the head simply because his wife, Lisa, wanted to be with her girlfriend, Shelbi. Lisa and Shelbi wished to remove Kevin from their lives. Lisa left the front door unlocked at Shelbi's request so that George, the driver Joe rode with, could enter the house and kill Kevin. He did it as a favor to Shelbi. Joe told me he did not know George would commit murder, but he knew something terrible was about to happen when George reached into the glove compartment and grabbed a gun before exiting the vehicle. George ran back to the car after shooting Kevin in his bed, and then he and Joe drove away while another friend sat in the backseat.

Later, while in jail, George shared the details with an attorney, leading authorities to monitor all parties involved. Shelbi suspected that George had snitched, so once he was out on bail, Shelbi told Joe and the guy in the backseat to fetch George and take him to a location where she waited for them. George had murdered Kevin as a favor for Shelbi, and now she wanted him dead. I recall Joe saying that once they arrived at the area where Shelbi waited that night, Shelbi shot George in the head. The backseat passenger was sentenced to just three years in exchange for his testimony against Joe, Shelbi, and Lisa. Lisa was sentenced to 25 years to life. Shelbi received 25 years to life plus life without parole. Joe received 50 years plus life without parole.

§

After not speaking to Joe since before COVID-19, I next encountered his voice through my television. In March 2023, I happened upon an episode of a gripping one-hour true crime series, "Mastermind of Murder." This show takes an in-depth look at women who, though physically detached from committing horrendous acts, are the sinister puppeteers behind a crime. The moment the show started, I was transfixed by the crime scene photos and the horrific details of crimes committed by Joe, George, Shelbi, Lisa, and the man in the backseat--Terence.

Narrating this harrowing tale was the detective assigned to their case. My disbelief was palpable as Joe's mugshot, an 18-year-old incarnation stripped of his familiar thick glasses and reddish facial hair, flashed on my screen. An audio recording was played. The detective asked Joe to provide a statement at the station, with his response being a plea to keep his name out of the case. I knew that voice, though I had not heard it in years.

Shelbi was the mastermind, but the detective made no bones about who wielded the gun—it was Joe. I recall that Joe had contacted George's family a few years ago to confess and apologize for being the shooter, but he told me he only did that to provide them with some semblance of closure. I believed him. I had never known Joe as a liar.

The students of my Prison Industrial Complex course wanted to meet him, so I sent a letter to ask him if he would speak with them. In the letter, I asked if he murdered his friend. We soon began messaging each other. He had a tablet, so we no longer had to write letters and wait a week for each other to know our feelings. In one of his messages, he admitted that he did, in fact, pull the trigger. He explained that he and Terence had planned to kill Shelbi, but then things got funky, and *he* ended up shooting George.

I forgave him for the lie. The man he has become, now 44 years old, is worthy of forgiveness. To openly declare such might come across as disrespectful to George's loved ones, and I am acutely aware of that. I feel uneasy about how my compassion for him may harm the families of those left behind.

§

I realize that our lives are shaped by the people we encounter, the relationships we form, and the lessons we learn along the way. Writing about him is my way of processing and reflecting upon those experiences and, perhaps, in some small way, forgiving myself for not being what he needed for the long haul.

I often find myself thinking about the bittersweet memories of our time together, the kindness we once expressed, and the painful words that drove us apart for years on multiple occasions. He and I message each other regularly now and express kindness and mutual respect. I hope he is able to find love someday, perhaps in the free world where I'm confident he will thrive.

HURT PEOPLE HURT PEOPLE

The kids who need the most love will ask for it
in the most unloving ways.

Russell Barkley

More than a decade ago, when I was in my early 40s, I
decided to spend time with a married couple searching for a
"unicorn"—a single bisexual woman open to joining couples
as a casual partner. Diego and Debra's profile read like a
fairytale romance, childhood best friends who reunited after
30 years and fell head over heels in love. The image of him
proposing on one knee with a diamond ring gave the
impression of them being happy, secure, and deeply in love.
I wasn't seeking a committed partnership but was open to
seeing them occasionally. We engaged in online and phone

conversations for over a week before I made the 90-minute journey to spend the night. I should have anticipated that things could sometimes get complicated.

While she often displayed self-deprecating humor and didn't have a formal education or job, she had a lovely personality. Her skin was a medium brown shade similar to mine, and her short hair rested smoothly on her flawless skin. She greeted me at the door in a t-shirt and denim jeans that were unbuttoned—as I would later notice she frequently wore—because of her protruding belly, much like mine and that of all the women on my father's side of the family, which made wearing tight-waisted jeans uncomfortable. I was not attracted to her, but physical attraction was not a significant factor for me. Debra was a woman of mild vibrancy in her forties who moved to Sacramento because Diego told her to leave her abusive husband and take the next train to be with him. The two had not seen each other in almost 30 years and were newlyweds, married six months after re-linking. Debra had found them a gorgeous two-bedroom apartment in a newer subdivision using her Section 8 government voucher. Her source of income was the disability check she received due to an autoimmune disease, resulting in occasional body aches.

Diego said he was a day laborer, though I had doubts. I never saw him work during the three months I knew them. He was obsessive about cleanliness and remained awake until dawn each day to clean the apartment, a habit I soon discovered was a remnant of his not-so-long-ago prison days. Diego was a burly, half-Black, half-Puerto Rican man, tall and tattooed. He wore a sculpted, thin-lined goatee along his chin and jawline. His broad shoulders were angled on his A-frame, and I could tell Debra's fine cooking was responsible for the new fat around his waist.

"He is my best friend, and I love everything about him." Her eyes brightened each time she mentioned him.

"I love my wife. My goal in life is to do whatever it takes to make her happy." While we were having dinner, Diego and Debra gazed at each other from across the table, their lips curled into smiles. Their expressions felt genuine to me.

Couples who invite others into their primary relationship require a solid foundation, so their reassurance that they were deeply in love was paramount. I didn't want to be part of a messy situation.

Following the meal, I mentioned my volunteer work with prisoners and shared my desire to write a book about my experiences with individuals I've known in prison.

"Hmph. I could tell you a thing or two about people in prison," he remarked in a hushed tone.

"Oh, really?" I responded with keen interest.

He then disclosed that he had been freed 18 months prior to our encounter after serving 13 years for murder. He was initially given a life sentence with no chance of parole for killing a man in an incident he justified as a drug deal that went bad. Later, he said it was self-defense.

As the night progressed, we drank, watched music videos, and engaged in "playful activities." Afterward, Diego went to the kitchen to clean. Debra propped up on an elbow and said, "When we were kids, Diego was a real troublemaker. I could never have imagined marrying him, not in a million years," she noted, her eyes sparkling. "Boys in our neighborhood would lie and say they had sex with me. Diego would fight them because he knew I was still a virgin. That was the first time I fell in love with him."

Debra and Diego rekindled their love soon after his

release from prison. They were still newlyweds, and I liked that they were sexually free, passionate, and willing to share. After dinner and a few drinks, I stayed overnight. I woke to Debra's bacon, eggs, toast, and hot tea. Over breakfast, I told him I was curious about his newfound freedom from prison, though I half-jokingly cautioned him that he might end up in my book.

"I would be honored to be immortalized in a book." His lopsided grin grew more pronounced.

When we met again after two weeks, Debra mentioned that he was enthusiastic and could not stop talking about seeing his story in print. She warned him not to get too roused, as the depiction might not be entirely favorable given how turbulent his life had been. I reiterated that whatever I wrote would not solely focus on him. It would be centered on the story we created together.

§

Diego's childhood was a torrent of pain and suffering. At two and a half years old, while his uncle was three, they played outside in a parked car. When Diego accidentally shifted the gear into neutral, a tire rolled over his uncle's skull. Overwhelmed by the anguish of her son's death, Diego's grandmother turned him and his sister over to the system, where he and his younger sister remained for six months before being accepted into a permanent foster home. Taken in by a woman he referred to as "my abuser," he lived with her from ages 3 to 13. Big Mama (as he initially called her) beat Diego daily, blaming him for random things like when the family cat gave birth to kittens in his bedroom dresser drawer. According to Diego, she would tie him up, beat the bottoms of his feet, and force him to strip naked to whip him. I was stunned. Diego lifted his shirt to reveal a raised scar on his lower back, a permanent welt from a racecar track toy that Big Mama had used to beat him.

In another conversation, Diego revealed that he had been arrested and held for a few hours when he was only eight. He shared that he had been falsely accused of multiple things, including stealing jewelry, having inappropriate relationships with Big Mama's granddaughter, trespassing in a neighbor's house, and stealing a dog. He adamantly denied any wrongdoing and attributed the accusations to neighbors, his abuser, and children who barely knew him.

Following an eight-month stay in a juvenile facility at the age of 13 for punching Big Mama in the mouth, Diego returned to the streets and embarked on a life of crime. He pimped women and maintained stash houses for his drugs, money, and weapons. He later joined a gang and fathered close-in-age children with various women.

Fighting was never a problem for Diego. He recounted a violent assault he once committed, for which he has no remorse. Calvin, Big Mama's son, had raped Diego years earlier. In 1994, he confronted Calvin at the high school where Calvin worked. His prideful recounting of exacting revenge sounded menacing, and one side of his mouth furrowed. I imagined Diego's eyes smoldering with a potent cocktail of anger and betrayal on the day he confronted Calvin at his job.

"Why did you do that shit to me?" Calvin called the police, who promptly escorted Diego off campus. But Diego was not done yet. He waited for the school day to end before following Calvin. Diego exacted his vengeance with a baseball bat, leaving Calvin for dead. His voice was unnervingly detached as he recounted this chilling tale to me. His words carried no hint of regret or remorse, just a bleak, matter-of-fact tone.

During one of our phone conversations during a week I did not see them, Diego confessed to committing assaults in prison, including stabbing and fighting, as a means to climb the ranks of the notorious Bloods gang. He spoke vaguely about specific acts of violence he had engaged in while in prison, justifying them as self-defense or in line with prison politics. He explained that he once spent two years in solitary confinement. As I listened to Diego's stories, I was torn. I felt sympathy for the abuse he had endured, and his involvement in a life of crime seemed understandable, considering his troubled childhood. However, I also questioned how a man with such significant trauma could sustain a healthy marriage and whether my presence in their relationship was a welcomed addition to their open, honest communication and well-established boundaries.

Although his biological mother lived next door, his abuser would physically assault him whenever he attempted to communicate with her through the shared fence. Eventually, his mom moved away and started a new family without Diego and his sister, leaving him feeling abandoned and betrayed. Diego's father was incarcerated during the first six years of Diego's life for his involvement in the Ñeta Association, a Puerto Rican gang. He spoke fondly of the Ñeta and insisted I view a YouTube video about the gang.

§

Seeing Diego's prison tattoo of his son's name on his upper arm prompted me to inquire. After serving eight years of his prison term for murder and resigning himself to a life behind bars, Diego received word that his 18-year-old son had been stabbed 26 times in a Sacramento park bathroom. Diego was locked in solitary confinement on the day of his son's murder, which, coincidentally, was his own 39th birthday. He described exercising outside in a stand-alone cage used for prisoners in solitary confinement when an officer approached him for a visit. He was surprised to see his then-wife and eldest son both somber and distressed. Overcome with emotion, they dropped the news.

Diego had shared fragments of the story. One day, I asked if he would be willing to share the complete story. He vividly described his experience, from the foreboding birthday to the grueling exercise routine on a scorching August day that seemed unnervingly silent and the grave tone of the officer who came to escort him from the exercise cage to his cell to prepare for a visit. He detailed his meticulous grooming in his cell. Despite the discomfort of his shackled hands and feet, his primary focus was on the mystery of why someone had arrived to visit him on a weekday. Upon entering the room, the subdued expressions on his son's and ex-wife's faces conveyed a profound message.

I took deep breaths as he disclosed that three thugs had orchestrated a plan to seek revenge on his son for a crime he had not committed.

"They lied on my son, Nandi. They killed him for nothing." He began weeping uncontrollably.

Debra stroked his head, arms, and back. The emotions became more intense. I reiterated my belief that it was not his fault. I could sense that he rarely cried, and I reassured him that his willingness to confront and experience those heart-wrenching emotions was a positive sign of emotional health. I offered words of comfort and solace.

She interrupted, saying, "Nandi, that's enough. This conversation is over." When he went to the bathroom, she explained that he had gotten to that part of the story many times, reacted the same way each time, and was likely to be in an unpleasant mood for a few days.

"I gotta be in this house by myself with him. I can't." I understood, so I called it a night.

I spoke to her on the phone the next day. Debra explained that things had escalated into a volatile situation between them. They argued throughout the night, and she blamed me for setting it off. Our three-way link had morphed into one in which I mediated their conflicts.

The next time I saw them was on a brief Sacramento visit to visit another friend. I told them I would stop by on my way back out of town. Upon my arrival, I found Debra secluded in her bedroom while Diego sat on the couch with his new black kitten, and both appeared somewhat distant and unwelcoming.

"What's going on?" I asked.

"You know what?" His body tensed, and his eyes took on a frighteningly aggressive expression. "You came in here and picked at some shit I was dealing with just fine." Aggrieved, he added that nudging him about his son was akin to the rape committed by Calvin.

I was speechless." Do you even care what people are going through?" His tone sounded more accusatory than inquisitive. Absolutely, I cared.

He frequently sought my opinion on various topics but demanded that I "leave all that sociology textbook stuff out. Just be yourself and answer the question." However, as soon as I opened my mouth to speak, he cut me off.

"Don't try to make me look stupid," he said, his voice filled with anger and resentment. I'm not as smart as you, but I'm not stupid."

Shocked, I was unable to respond. It felt like I was on

trial, forced to defend myself against some invisible accusation. My palms grew sweaty, and my throat felt dry. I was suffocating under the weight of his words.

He continued his impassioned rant. "You're either a victim or a victimizer. I ain't gonna let nobody victimize me." Despite my sympathy for the story he had shared regarding his son and witnessing the raw emotions he expressed, I simply nodded as he continued his tirade. He then questioned whether I understood anything he was saying. At some point, Debra emerged from the back and silently mouthed that he was drunk. Diego added that "the system" refused to allow him to fully reintegrate into society after 18 months of being home from prison. He could not secure formal employment as evidence. Debra came from the back and mouthed that he was drunk.

"I'm just gonna go." I stood up and walked to the kitchen, where Debra was standing. I hugged her. As I headed toward the door, Diego approached me from behind, and his fingers clamped down on my arm with a forceful grip. He snatched my body around. I jerked my arm from his grasp and leered at him. My eyes narrowed.

His pupils flared. "How the fuck are you going to leave my house and hug my wife but not hug me? Then you have the fucking nerve to snatch your arm away from me?" I glanced in Debra's direction and walked out the door to my car. In the days that followed, Diego sent me multiple berating text messages. He nitpicked at the choice of words I had used in previous conversations, criticized the timing of returning a jacket I had borrowed, and even commented on how little I laughed in his presence. Occasionally, he made derogatory remarks about my femininity and belittled his wife for behaving like me during the rare times she asserted herself.

§

Debra and I met for coffee at Barnes and Noble in Sacramento the following week. She arrived with a black eye, bruises on the left side of her face, a limp, and rib pain. She insisted she had instigated a fight with Diego.

Debra didn't want to tell me what had happened the night before. She did, however, mention that Diego had an affair with a clerk from the grocery store, and the woman had knocked on their door searching for the Puerto Rican man she had been seeing. There were also two instances when he disappeared for days, including one time he took out the garbage and returned a week later. At the time of our coffee date, she hadn't seen him for two days.

After talking briefly, she expressed her desire for me to teach her how to read. I gladly accepted her request and thought doing so would help us build a new friendship. I grabbed an Essence magazine from a rack and said, "Let's check out what's happening in the world of Black women." I placed the magazine in front of her to gauge her reading level. Her finger shyly tapped the glossy pages as she delicately pointed to one word at a time. However, she struggled and mispronounced many of the words. Her shoulders trembled, and tears began streaming down her face.

"It's okay, Sis." We can try again later." I offered a soft, half grin, and I placed my hand on top of hers.

"Nobody wanna take the time to teach me. Thank you, Nandi." We leaned into each other, and our cheeks rested together.

Then she asked me to help with their bills and said Diego had money coming and he would pay me back in exactly one week. I gave her cash, and we went our separate ways.

I messaged both of them a week later about my money. Debra informed me that she didn't have it. Then she added, "Stay away from my husband." She made it clear that they had nothing else to say to me. I wasn't sure what he had said to her or what kind of scheme they might have devised together, but I knew they were going to repay me. I messaged them a few more times, and they ignored me.

The following week, I was in Sacramento for a show. I appeared at their front door unannounced. He opened the door and stunk of strong liquor. She was not home. I told him I was there for my money. He reluctantly wrote me two checks and told me to cash them on different days. However, when I went to his bank on Monday morning, they informed me that his account had been closed for months. I was fed up. Frustrated, I messaged him that writing bad checks was a felony that could land him back in prison. In response, he requested that I drive to their place in Sacramento, return the checks, and sign an agreement saying I wouldn't press charges. I firmly refused.

"You have 24 hours to deposit my money into my bank account, or I will turn these bad checks over to the police," I warned. Although I had no intention of involving the police or having him arrested over the checks, my threat sounded genuine enough. He deposited my money that same day.

§

Three years later, I entered a Chinese restaurant a few blocks from my house. Out of the corner of my eye, I glimpsed Debra seated with a beautiful brown woman. My stomach sank, and I looked away, pretending not to notice her. Questions flooded my mind. Did she involve me in their drama, knowing he was a ticking time bomb? Were they still together? Was he back in prison? Some things were better left unasked and unsaid.

§

Unicorns sometimes encounter unique situations, like storms brewing on the horizon or forest paths that lead to nowhere. Debra and Diego were a turbulent duo who left me longing for calmer seas and clearer skies. People who leave behind a trail of chaos in their wake feel like a never-ending game of Russian roulette, with each encounter bringing the possibility of disaster.

Because of them, I resolved to steer clear of any tempests that might arise, choosing instead to seek solace in simple, solitary pleasures.

BURNT BRIDGES

My daughter, when I told her of our topic and
my difficulty with it, said, 'Tell them about
how you're never really a whole person if you
remain silent, because there's always that one
little piece inside you that wants to be spoken
out, and if you keep ignoring it, it gets madder
and madder and hotter and hotter, and if you
don't speak it out one day it will just up and
punch you in the mouth from the inside.

Audre Lorde

In 2008 or 2009, I came across Saad's ad on a prisoner
pen pal website. Something about his warm and friendly tone
immediately caught my attention. He was looking for socially

conscious folks—including professors—who wanted to have deep conversations about religion, social issues, and life. After a week of consideration, I decided to write to him. I didn't know what to expect from our correspondence, but as usual, I was intrigued by the idea of getting to know someone living a life different from my own.

Saad was just a year younger than me. A devout Muslim, he spent most of his days in prayer and mentoring other Muslims. He tried to convert me to Islam, often sounding like a salesman describing the best features of the religion. I was initially open, but many of his conservative views, especially the ones about women, did not appeal to me. He was ambitious to learn about my views and began calling himself a feminist based on discussions we had.

Before he embraced religion in prison, Saad had enjoyed life on the streets. His most notable crime—a botched getaway—landed him a 28-year sentence. He'd paid an addict $20 to borrow a car, only to be pulled over with weed and stolen electronics inside. In his dramatic YouTube retelling, he jumped from a bridge in a desperate bid to flee, breaking half the bones in his body when he hit the asphalt. The incident left him wheelchair-bound for three years, but he eventually regained mobility—walking with a crooked hip and flashing a set of dazzling veneers. He described the ordeal as follows:

> It was easily the worst day of my life. I was pulled over by the highway patrol. I had some marijuana on me and didn't want to get caught with it, so I pulled over with the sole intent of trying to just get away from him and get rid of it. Once I got rid of the weed, I still planned on not going to jail.

I [saw a traffic sign] on the right shoulder of the freeway and crossed the left shoulder. I thought I was up and over the center divider, but I wasn't. Before I looked to see where I was going, I jumped over the cement barriers and quickly realized I was falling over a bridge. By the time I was able to process that I was falling over, I was hitting the ground at the same time. I impacted the asphalt—not dirt, not water, not grass, but asphalt. I just laid there on my back.

I saw two officers shining a light down on me and telling me not to move. If I could have, I would have. Cars driving by could have easily run me over as I lay in the street. I started having images flash in my head from when I was five, six, ten, and a teenager. The last image was my mom crying, and then I fell unconscious.

I woke up handcuffed and leg-chained to a hospital bed. Every single joint and bone hurt as I lay in that bed. I broke my left arm. I broke my femur bone, the largest and strongest bone in your body. I broke it in five places. I broke my right hip, I broke my jaw, and I knocked out some teeth.

After a year of exchanging letters and phone calls, I started visiting Saad at a prison 2.5 hours away. He always wore a crocheted kufi, a modest head covering, just like the one in his pen pal ad. He had one in every color. On his birthday one year, I joined his sister, brother-in-law, and niece for a visit. It was clear his sister was his best friend, their love for each other palpable. Though his mother couldn't visit often, Saad cherished their bond and often said his post-prison plans revolved around making her proud.

§

One visit sticks out for its sheer absurdity. I had dressed in all white, forgetting that visitors weren't allowed to wear the color—prisoners in medical or disciplinary units also wore white. With only three hours left for visitation, I had two options: change into clothes from a nearby trailer or rush to Ross to buy something new. After a wild goose chase trying to locate the trailer, I opted for Ross. By the time I returned, another woman strolled in wearing head-to-toe white, unbothered and unchallenged. I vented my frustration to Saad, who simply said, "That's how it is around here." It was a crash course in the maddening arbitrariness of prison rules.

Despite having visited Saad numerous times, my interest in him remained strictly platonic. However, Saad repeatedly proposed marriage to me, explaining that, as a Muslim, he didn't believe in dating. Instead, he believed in connecting with a Muslimah, marrying her, and then developing love within the marriage. Saad attempted to convert me to his faith, but I was content with my own spiritual journey, which leans more toward Buddhism. Saad hoped that we could marry and have the privacy of conjugal visits to foster love, but I respectfully declined all his proposals.

Then one day, he informed me that he had developed a connection with a Canadian woman. Although they hadn't met in person, she had agreed to marry him. However, their long-distance relationship fizzled when she couldn't afford to visit him.

§

By spring 2011, Saad played a pivotal role in my "Prison Industrial Complex" course. He connected my students with incarcerated men willing to correspond and share their stories. The students' essays about these interactions were raw and unpolished, but I kept my promise to compile them into a self-published book. Saad was thrilled to be part of it, calling it a testament to his ability to create something positive while incarcerated.

On the first day of that semester, I promised the class that I would self-publish their final essays, which thrilled them. However, by the end of the semester, when they were tired and unmotivated, their work required an overwhelming number of edits, and the quality was not great. I titled the book *Whispers Over the Wall* and self-published it on Amazon. (It's not that good, so don't rush to get it.)

§

Saad and I often found ourselves on opposite sides of the fence when discussing social justice issues, particularly those at the intersection of gender, race, and sex. I urged him to expand his perspective beyond Islam. For Saad, there was nothing beyond Islam. My opinions are shaped by the teachings of sociologists, extensive reading, primary research, and the perspectives of my colleagues and students. On the other hand, Saad's views were derived from the Qur'an, books that resonated with socially- and freedom-conscious men in prison, as well as his own observations of his environment. This is not to say that my views were correct or that he was mistaken. The gaps in our agreement merely stemmed from his limited access to reliable resources, my limited knowledge of Islam, and our unique life experiences.

Saad and I debated fundamental issues. For instance, we discussed his firm belief that it was unjust for prisons to release individuals without providing them with a place to live. He felt that individuals should be allowed to remain in prison if they had no alternative housing options.

He passionately argued, "You can't just toss people onto the streets with no support. A man who's spent most of his life behind bars, and then he's just kicked out with nowhere to go? That's just wrong."

"Saad, prisons aren't meant to be homeless shelters. I agree it's heartbreaking when ex-prisoners end up with nowhere to go, but we can't use prisons as a solution to homelessness." I suggested that prison structures could be repurposed, similar to abandoned malls, as safe havens for the unhoused, where they could find respite from harsh weather, access necessary resources for an effective transition, and enjoy the freedom of movement. That's just me imagining. Our debates were always respectful. Although I frequently disagreed with Saad, there was a certain appeal to how he expressed his opinions. He was passionately open to discussion. We respected each other's viewpoints and saw these exchanges as opportunities for learning and growth.

§

Like other prisoners, Saad managed to acquire cell phones. I didn't ask how he obtained them, but it was an open secret that some correctional officers were involved in smuggling them inside. He informed me that the devices came at a steep price, ranging from $800 to $1200. One of his friends held the phone during the day, and Saad had it in the evenings. We occasionally connected through video chat, and I caught glimpses of his daily life in the dorms, with his feet propped up on a desk while he was at work. On several occasions, officers discovered the phone, but Saad always managed to get a new one. The Canadian woman may have bought one for him, and his sister and mom probably helped with the others.

After persistent requests, Saad was eventually transferred to San Quentin, a prison known for its wide range of educational services. He found success with The Last Mile, a program that taught him. Saad gained the ability to develop digital solutions, enabling him to express his creativity and problem-solving skills. The Last Mile program gave him a sense of purpose and a marketable skill that could lead to employment after his release.

By 2017, we had drifted apart. Then, out of the blue, Saad called to tell me he'd been released. Coincidentally, I was in Sacramento that day and visited him at his grandmother's house. When I arrived, he greeted me outside, still wearing a kufi, warmly referring to me as "Sista," as he always did, and flashing his vibrant veneers. His grandmother was delightfully hilarious. The three of us spent about an hour together and took a few photos before I left.

When he walked me to my car, I told him my students would love to hear his story. A couple of weeks later, I secured a small amount of funding from the university to bring Saad as a guest speaker. While touring the campus, he remarked how mind-blowing it was to see so many women wearing leggings, as it made them appear nearly naked. He found it distracting and immodest.

He spoke to three of my classes in one day, including my women's studies course. His story intrigued most of my students. During his talk, Saad referred to himself as a feminist, explaining that he believed in women's rights. I had already explained to him over the years that contemporary feminism encompasses more than just rights, especially for marginalized people. His ideas about women sparked lively conversations among my students, with some questioning how he reconciled his strict views on gender roles as a Muslim. Some students were skeptical, while others were fascinated by and fixated on his transition from prisoner to "regular guy." Despite differing opinions, Saad's visit sparked a heightened interest in the issues he raised. Between classes, we walked around campus and took lots of photos.

Afterward, I treated him to dinner at Applebee's. However, he and his new ex-wife, Crystal, started arguing through text messages while we were eating. They had been "Islamically" married for a couple of months but had just broken up. Throughout the day, he talked to me about her dirty house and unruly child. Then he began showing me their text messages at the restaurant, later in the car, and when we arrived at my house. I felt like I was watching a car crash in slow motion. They were fully engaged in an argument when we arrived. He forwarded the entire thread so I could see just how awful she was. I was shocked by both of them. Below is their verbatim exchange:

> **Crystal**: (The message had a photo of a man attached.) This is the man I am going to marry. Insha'Allah, I will be moving to Baltimore next summer. However, we plan to get married Islamically immediately and get pregnant. Enjoy your life, Saad.

> **Saad**: He can have your materialistic ass.

Probably the only one who will take you with all your emotional baggage and insecurities. I do not need that burden. You are not the last woman on Earth. Certainly not the finest. I trust in Allah. He will send me someone. Hopefully, a natural beauty that does not wear fake hair, fake nails, fake eyes, just fake all around. Give me a real woman with natural attributes. Not someone posting her old pics trying to cling on to her former glory. I have seen you undressed, unkempt, and after getting drilled.

Crystal: Nah nigga! Men have never stopped wanting me. That is what pisses you off. Even while you were in the picture, they were there. Faggot.

Saad: They can have your obese ass. They do not really want you, either. If they did, they would have you. Keep telling yourself that, though. Remember, I have seen you naked, how you look today. Not in some old-ass pics from 5-10 years ago. You are way past your prime. Quit trying to hold on to old glory. You used to be all that. Now all you are is a bag of chips.

Crystal: I'm freshly fucked and lying in his bed. Lmao. He does not allow me to wear makeup or fake hair with him. SMH.

Saad: You go right ahead and keep trying to

convince yourself that these men still want you. Psychological warfare is kickin' your ass right along with the Shaytan. It is fitting for what you have become.

Crystal: Note who said 'I love you' first.

Saad: I have fucked you enough to not be jealous. Pussy is a dime a dozen. Yours is good, but I will not miss it. Wait 'til he sees the wig, makeup, and girdle come off. Your pics are altered, filtered, and just masks. I fell for it. I can see that he will, too.

Crystal: I have a real man. Not a weak ass li'l boy bitch like yourself!

Saad: Go get him, then. That's if he even wants you, which I doubt. Bye, heifer!!!

The venom in his words shocked me. This wasn't the Saad I thought I knew. My stomach churned as I watched his resentment unfold in real time, wondering if our friendship would someday turn the same shade of bitterness.

A month later, he messaged me about not answering one of his calls, and then sent the following message:

Wow! You flipped on me quickly. Very well. Just chalk it up to the insecurities and intelligence of yet another scarred, angry Black woman who thinks everything is a man's fault. I thought you were bigger than that. I thought we were better than that. I guess you were faking it all along. You are just like those other women. I should've known.

I am unsure how I got lumped in with "those other women" after we had been kind to each other for years.

"Thank you," I replied.

"You're not welcome. Good riddance!" Saad wrote back.

If he had embraced the information I shared, including the books I sent him about women's issues, rather than a simplistic version of the movement focused on rights, he would have known how anti-feminist it is to attack women's bodies, our strength, and perpetuate stereotypes about Black women being angry. He had never commented on me thinking everything was a man's fault, and I wasn't even aware of why he felt that. Why couldn't I have simply been someone who hadn't responded to messages? How did he conclude that I had been faking being nice for 10 years?

In my final expression to him, I typed, "Please do not contact me again. I'm asking this respectfully, and I hope you will honor my wish." I don't stick around for very long when sugar turns to shit.

Within an hour, Saad emailed me again, saying, "I retract the words of my last email. Your friendship means way too much to me to just let it go. Please tell me what it was that touched a nerve for you and educate me as you always have. Your words matter, Nandi. You matter. I am sorry. Please respond." I didn't.

Not long after, another nasty message arrived. My phone continued to ping with messages from Saad, each with a different plea or ugly sentiment. That was the last time I allowed Saad access to my life. Weeks later, I deleted his wedding invitation without hesitation. The chapter of Saad was closed, and with it, any tolerance for the chaos he brought.

Some connections are valuable for the lessons they leave behind, even if they're painful. Saad taught me about resilience, but also about boundaries—the kind you draw to protect your peace. His story will always linger in my mind, not as a cautionary tale, but as a reminder: you don't have to light yourself on fire to keep someone else warm.

Besides, I'm too old for nonsense.

BENEATH THE INK

Friendship is so weird. You just pick a human
you've met and you're like, 'Yep, I like this
one,' and you just do stuff with them.

Bill Murray

I found Keith's ad on a prisoner pen pal site. His photo
lacked warmth. No hint of a smile. His gaze was pensive and
intense, his hands clasped. Beneath his right eye was a star
tattoo, bold and unmissable.

Curious, I sent him one of my calls for submissions to a
book project I dreamed of—stories from people with facial
tattoos. I cast a wide net: tattoo shops, physicians known for
removals, prisoners advertising online. Among the
responses, Keith's essay about his daughter stood out. It was

raw, poignant, and teeming with longing. I suggested he expand the story into a standalone autobiography.

We began as pen pals, exchanging occasional letters. However, as our connection deepened, I shared my phone number, and our relationship evolved into regular phone conversations. I often imagined him leaning against a cinderblock wall beneath a mounted phone whenever he called me. With each call, it felt like a window into a world drastically different from mine. Sometimes, I could hear the sound of clanging metal doors and the murmur of distant voices echoing from the tier. We teased each other and shared laughter. I found myself eagerly anticipating his weekly calls.

Keith frequently spoke about his daughter. He had fallen in love with a prison nurse, and the two began a secret relationship. She became pregnant with his daughter but was terminated from her job shortly after. Despite this setback, Keith and the nurse maintained contact for a brief period, and she visited him periodically. When his daughter was five years old, she shared a heartbreaking sentiment, expressing how she looked at the stars every night, imagining that her daddy was one of them, watching over her from afar. The profound sweetness of her words melted Keith's heart.

Keith's star tattoo, placed under his eye, was a physical reminder of his love for his daughter. Years had passed since he last heard from his daughter or her mother when we met, but the star tattoo remained a daily symbol of his unwavering love. Reading his submission detailing this story filled me with a surge of sadness.

§

Keith's life took a tragic turn when he was just 11 years

old. He suffered a brutal beating from his stepfather that left him hospitalized with a collapsed lung. As a result, Keith's mother lost custody of him, and he spiraled. It seemed like Keith's destiny was sealed. After numerous stints in different institutions, he ended up sentenced to 284 years. His path was paved early, and it ended with a 284-year sentence. His most significant crime was the murder of his mother's boyfriend, Bill.

In 1994, Keith's mother was in a relationship with Bill, an alcoholic who often beat her. According to public legal documents, on the night of the murder, Bill was drunk, had sexually assaulted Keith's mom, and threatened to kill her if she left. She rushed to a pay phone and begged Keith to come over. When he arrived, she told her son to stab Bill while he slept, a thought that made him rush outside and vomit. She then gave her son Bill's gun, and Keith shot him in the neck and head.

For her role in the murder, Keith's mother served 21 years before reentering the free world without a word of apology or support for her son.

§

Keith and I share little in terms of identities or backstories. I'm a Black woman with no criminal history, and he is a White man who once embraced violence and hatred. He was also a self-proclaimed racist. Keith had been a member of the Aryan Brotherhood, proudly wearing "White Pride" tattooed across his neck. Unlike prisoners who join racist gangs out of survival, Keith believed in the ideologies. He studied Hitler's teachings.

But Keith's allegiance to the Brotherhood ended in 2002. They ordered him to kill a fellow member—a friend—and when he refused, they put out a hit on him. Keith chose survival. He debriefed with the California Department of Corrections, disavowed the gang, and testified against them in a federal case. This act severed him from his old life forever. Currently, he is serving his sentence on a sensitive needs yard (SNY) alongside thousands of other men in California who have left gangs behind.

Keith dedicated himself to self-improvement. He tutored other prisoners pursuing their GEDs and trained service dogs. He distanced himself from prison politics and embraced a quieter, purpose-driven existence.

§

In 2015, while Keith grappled with the news of his mother's release, I offered to visit him. He had been hurt by her abandonment—five years without contact, no apology. I wanted to show him kindness, to sit across from him and offer my presence. But when I asked for a visitor's application, Keith brushed me off.

"Send me the form," I said again a month later, hopeful.

Instead of sending the application, Keith stopped calling. It would be nearly two years before I heard from him again.

His letter, when it came, began with:

"Hello there, stranger! I cannot remember the last time I wrote, but I never received a response, which broke my heart. I hope I never said or did anything to hurt or upset you. I hope you will contact me ASAP—I have worried about you, and I am right here for you! I still believe in my heart that your coming into my life encouraged me to do such great things."

By then, I had married, and my spouse wasn't comfortable with my prison friendships. I wrote sparingly, unsure how to navigate the boundaries of my new life.

Some people might find it odd for a woman of color to form a bond with a man who had been a white supremacist. However, I enjoy connecting with people from all walks of life, so our connection felt like a natural expression of myself. Surprisingly, race, a topic one might expect to be significant, rarely came up in our many phone conversations. Laughter became our shared language as we joked about our everyday lives. I typically do not banter with people because my feelings are hurt easily; sometimes, I take a humorous dig too seriously. Keith and I bantered often, and it always felt safe.

Keith would talk about his daughter, whom he deeply missed, and we'd discuss small and significant victories in our lives. He also expressed his passion for books and the courses he was taking to improve himself. Our interactions were always supportive and kind.

Keith was, and still is, an extraordinarily intelligent person teeming with potential. The tattoos he once proudly wore as symbols of racial hatred are now a source of shame. It was evident that he had a troubled past, but as I got to know him better, I was impressed with his life-changing decision to leave all that behind and strive for a better life despite the risks involved. Whenever I asked Keith about his life and experiences in prison, he consistently displayed patience and openness. His focus on self-improvement showed me that he was not defined by the person he used to be. I appreciated his support and encouragement, as he genuinely cared about the events in my life and my work.

On the surface, our friendship may have seemed like an unlikely pairing, but there was something about our willingness to connect on a human level that allowed us to be vulnerable with each other. We found common ground through our shared experiences. Sometimes, the most unexpected individuals have the most captivating and transformative stories. When our paths first crossed, I couldn't help but be drawn to the star tattoo beneath his eye because of my project, which never came to fruition. As his friend, I discovered the depth of his story by getting to know the man beneath the ink. Bonding with him proved that two people from unique backgrounds can find common ground and form a meaningful connection.

Keith reached out to me in the fall of 2020 with exciting news about his petition for a re-sentencing hearing, expressing joy in the positive direction his life has taken. He included a powerful note from other prisoners who had witnessed his growth. Early in 2023, I submitted a letter to Keith's attorney supporting his plea for a second chance at freedom.

Although we have never met in person, I got to know him a bit. He believes he can still make a positive impact on the world. And I think that about him, too. Befriending a former white supremacist may seem controversial to many people. There is something special about getting to know someone beyond their appearance, situation, and context—especially if we appear to be opposites. As someone who has always been fascinated by the capacity for transformation and growth, I found him intriguing.

When he detailed the abuse he suffered, I sort of understood his prior violent behavior and the sense of belonging he sought within a gang. While I could never condone the hateful beliefs and actions Keith once embraced, I was profoundly moved by his rejection of those ideas, that he made amends and embarked on a different path of empathy, understanding, and compassion. Some of Keith's tattoos are now covered, and he is currently on a list to have others removed.

§

Keith's transformation fascinated me. Here was a man who had once embraced hatred, now filled with remorse and yearning for redemption. His tattoos, once symbols of supremacy, had become marks of shame. He covered some and joined a waiting list to remove others.

When he spoke to my students in 2023 via video chat, some were skeptical. One student, a White woman with a mixed-race child, questioned whether Keith might still harbor his old prejudices. Others dismissed him outright: "Once a racist, always a racist."

I disagreed. People can change.

In an email to the student, I posed a hypothetical:

"Suppose I told you about a friend who, at 11, was beaten so badly by his stepfather that he spent weeks in the hospital. His mother lost custody, and he fell into juvie. At 19, she handed him a gun and begged him to kill the man who was beating her. And he did it.

Suppose I told you he would never leave prison because of that one act. Would your heart go out to him? At what point do we stop extending compassion to an 11-year-old boy with a collapsed lung? Does that moment pass the instant he violates our moral code?"

Keith taught me that redemption doesn't require perfection. People don't need to fit into neat boxes to be worthy of compassion. I've often felt torn, wondering why I continue to care for prisoners despite knowing the toll these relationships take. But I'm drawn to stories of transformation—stories like Keith's, where a man covered in hateful ink chooses to change.

He risked his life to disavow the Brotherhood. He testified against them. He walked away from the ideologies that once consumed him. Now, he spends his days striving to make a positive impact.

Keith's life is a story of tragedy, love, loss, and growth. It is proof that even the most unlikely people can find redemption. His star tattoo—the mark that first drew me to him—will always remind me of his capacity for change and the beauty of believing in what's possible.

JOHNNY & JDP

The meaning of life is to find your gift. The
purpose of life is to give it away.

Pablo Picasso

Johnny and I had exchanged letters for over two years
when he asked Karen to invite me to Mule Creek State
Prison's Juvenile Diversion Program (JDP) in 2014. JDP
reminded me of *Scared Straight,* but without the yelling,
cursing, and threats. The men running the program brought
hard-earned lessons from their own lives, aiming to steer
kids away from choices that could land them in prison.

Karen, a vivacious Christian woman in her 70s, often
referred to the prisoners who ran the group as "my guys."
Even after she retired from her position in the Receiving and

Release Department of the prison at the start of COVID-19, she continued to serve as the program's volunteer coordinator. She was emotionally invested in the success of all her guys, a fact that was evident when she shared that Johnny, one of the program facilitators, wanted me to join them.

"Johnny really wants you to see this," she told me.

I had learned about Johnny when he submitted an essay, "Cutting Ties," to my edited volume, *This Side of My Struggle*. The piece was about the homicide he committed at 16 as a gang member. A cab driver doubted his ability to pay for a ride and demanded to see cash. Johnny pulled a gun, there was a struggle, and the gun went off. The driver died, and Johnny ran.

Johnny's mother convinced him to turn himself in. He was sentenced to life in prison for homicide and spent nearly 30 years behind bars. By the time he reached out to me, his letters painted a picture of a man changed by time.

He wrote regularly—every few months, at first—to tell me about his life, his family, and the progress of his appeal. Occasionally, his letters included his personal drawings, which I still have and photos: Johnny seated next to his children, his parents flanking him, all smiles. Those visits, he said, were his brightest moments, right next to his work with JDP. Johnny included a visiting form in three letters, encouraging me to see him in person during regular weekend visiting hours. I suspected that he had developed an attraction for me. I was not interested in him that way, so I declined. Still, he insisted he wanted me to come solely for conversation.

Johnny correctly assumed that I would be eager to witness the outstanding work he and the other men did to empower kids. Consequently, I gladly accepted when Karen sent me an email inviting me to observe them. I ended up joining the group on multiple occasions.

§

A typical JDP Saturday began with Karen warmly greeting 5-10 teenage boys and their counselors in the check-in lobby. Some kids who promise to come don't show up, but those who do are unsure what to expect. The staff members who drive them to the facility, employed by non-profit organizations, often share the challenge of rousing kids early on Saturdays. Despite the commitment from the kids and their parents, when the counselors show up at their homes, they just don't want to wake up. Little do they know the gifts that await them at the prison.

The boys, aged 13 to 19, come from crime-ridden, gang-infested communities. They are given pink vests to ensure easy identification in chaotic situations. Some are familiar with each other or even related. Along with correctional officers, Karen escorts them from the lobby to the receiving area of the prison, where they are placed together in a cell. I accompanied the group and chatted with Karen while the juveniles entered the cell. Once inside, they lean against the cinderblock wall to appear confident. Their bodies are tense, and the display of confidence feels contrived. I observe from outside the cell, anticipating the men's arrival at any moment. Soon, a half dozen uniformed prisoners round the corner, enter the cell, and ask the boys how they feel. Some admit they are nervous. Other times, they look at the floor and lie.

"We'll show you respect. You show us respect, too," one of them said.

The boys nodded.

From there, the group moved to the education building. Karen explained the circle of chairs in the room: enough for the boys and their mentors, plus a few holding framed photos of kids who had come to the program in the past. The images were reminders of lives lost—some to prison, others to the streets.

The JDP men introduced themselves.

"My name is—, A12345. I'm here for murder. Been down since '98, and I'm never going home."

Each man shared his crime and sentence, voices heavy with regret.

When it was Johnny's turn, he said, "I was convicted of second-degree murder at age 16. I may never go home."

He caught my eye and smiled, a flicker of warmth in the heaviness of the moment.

Each JDP day consisted of breakout sessions, lunch, and a tour of the housing area. During the sessions, Johnny encouraged the boys to critically reflect on the connection between their behavior and their love for their families.

"You say you love your mother, right? How do you think your mother will feel having to visit you here for the rest of her life?" Johnny's questions for the boys were direct and piercing.

During lunch in the chow hall, after hours of conversation, the boys sit down for one-on-one discussions with their mentors, engaging in intimate conversations about their lives. They are served boxed lunches with white-bread sandwiches and cartons of warm milk. The one-on-one chats are private, and an inaudible murmur fills the chow hall. Karen, the sponsors, and outside guests talk among ourselves since we are not privy to mentor-mentee discussions.

§

When I returned nearly a year later, Johnny wasn't there.

"He's no longer part of the program," Karen told me with a sigh. "He started gambling and using drugs. He had to transfer to another yard."

Karen's disappointment cut through her words.

"Damn," I said. "I hope he gets his stuff together before he goes home."

"It's sad. He was doing so well. He even has a release date now. Many of these guys never get a second chance."

"Damn. I hope he gets his stuff under control before he goes home."

A few months later, I attended a non-JDP event at the prison. I spotted Johnny walking towards me in the open yard among hundreds of prisoners. As he got closer, I noticed the stark change in his appearance. He looked thin, and the features around his eyes were dark.

"Hey, Professor." He was pleasant and curious about why I was there.

"Hi, Johnny. Where have you been?" I already knew.

"I'm getting ready to go home. Oh, I wanted to give you a heads-up." He leaned in close to my one good ear. "Your home address was on the receipt for the books you sent me from Amazon." He spoke so softly that I asked him to repeat himself. I assumed he was warning me that several other men now had my home address since I had also sent them books from Amazon.

"Okay," I responded. "How come I didn't see you the last time I visited JDP?"

"I'll write to you and tell you all about it." He smiled and walked away. That was the last time I saw Johnny.

§

A week later, I received a letter in which he explained that he chose to walk away from JDP because the other guys envied his impending release. He didn't admit to using drugs or gambling, but I knew what Karen and the others told me was true. Johnny was released from prison soon after he mailed me that letter, in which he also promised to stay in touch. I did not hear from him again.

Five months later, I got an email from his fiancée:

> "Dr. Crosby, my name is Gina. I was engaged to Johnny from your book. I want to thank you for impacting Johnny's life. He mentioned you often. He came home on October 15, 2017, and struggled with being home and with the heroin addiction he fought while incarcerated. He overdosed and was laid to rest in March 2018.
>
> It has been challenging for all of us. As you may know, he reconnected with his children after almost a lifetime apart. It's a sad story because we also reconnected after 28 years of separation. He was doing amazing things when he came home. He had a job with the Carpenters Union, bought a car, and was living a seemingly normal life with me. I knew he was struggling, but I couldn't have imagined this. I think he wanted it all and maybe didn't realize how hard it would be. His family was very supportive while he was inside, but they also struggled with him being home because of what he did.
>
> He was very proud to be part of your book.

I read it, and it gave me some clarity about what truly happened. I will share it with some of the people he mentioned as positive influences. I was ready to spend at least another 40 years with him. So, my heart hurts too. His family, though supportive while he was inside, struggled with him being home because of his past actions. I had a miscarriage before he passed. We were devastated.

I have had losses in my life, but losing him has by far been the toughest thing I have had to deal with. I miss everything about him. Nights are the hardest of all.

Immediately, I sent a screenshot of the message to Karen. While she and her guys were not shocked, they were disappointed that Johnny squandered such a fantastic opportunity and saddened that he veered so far from the path.

§

JDP continued without Johnny. Andre, one of the facilitators, moved me deeply. He told the boys about the crime that put him in prison: how, at 19, he shot two people over a gang debt, killing one and paralyzing the other. Tears rolled down his face as he recounted the moment.

He held a role as a violent enforcer within his gang. While buying diapers for his three-year-old daughter, he received a call to collect money from someone who owed a debt. Instead of returning home, he drove to the young man's house, abducted his parents when he discovered the man wasn't there, and took them to an abandoned area where he shot them. One parent succumbed to their injuries, while the other was left paralyzed.

I watched as Andre had a powerful interaction with an 18-year-old JDP participant who was visiting for the second time, this time accompanied by his 14-year-old brother.

Andre recognized the young man's haircut as a sign of a gangbanger, so he called him out. "I know that haircut, man. You still bangin'. You told me you were ready to get away from those streets and be a role model for your little brother. If you're really ready, why don't you cut your hair?" He gestured to another prisoner to fetch scissors.

"I'll cut it when I get home." The young man hesitated, aware of the consequences he might face from his gang if he were to go home without the distinctive hairstyle. Tension filled the room as Andre pleaded with him to cut his hair. "If you meant everything you said today, you can cut it now." Andre stood towering over the seated boy, who was visibly uncomfortable with the request. A hush lingered in the room. The young man shifted in his chair but stood his ground and continued to say no.

"C'mon, Man. I'm begging you. Cut your hair." Andre's voice cracked.

The boy shook his head. "I just can't."

"Why not?" Andre pressed.

"It's my hair, man. I can't do it right now." He appeared to be weighing the long-term consequences. When someone handed Andre the scissors, he ramped up his insistence. "You and I both know why you won't cut it. Show your little brother that the streets have nothing to offer him, man."

We watched to see if the kid would grab the scissors. He did not. A flicker of hesitation danced across the youth's face as he responded, "I'll cut it when I get home," his voice quivering with apprehension. The weight of his decision pressed heavily upon him, acutely aware that returning without the long ponytail would brand him as a dropout and a traitor to his gang.

Andre's voice grew more intense, and his eyes narrowed in urgency. Andre became visibly emotional before walking from the middle of the circle toward the door where I was seated. He looked at me and choked out the words, "I failed."

"You did not fail, Brother. That was powerful. Would it be okay if I hugged you?"

He turned to the nearby officer and requested permission to hug me, which the officer granted with a slight nod. Andre and I embraced briefly. Looking into his eyes, I felt a mixture of compassion and frustration: compassion for Andre's attempts to help and frustration at a system that restricts small gestures of humanity between two consenting adults. This moment lingered with me for days.

§

During the conclusion of every JDP event, I hear heartfelt statements like "I love you, man," "I believe in you," and "I am proud of you." Some JDP men are fathers, while others are speaking to their younger selves. The boys sit next to their mentors while Karen stands at the edge of the circle, closest to the door, holding the photographs that had been propped up in chairs throughout the day. She expresses gratitude to the men, offers well wishes for the youth, and thanks the sponsors for their dedication.

A couple of the kids who once participated in the program were murdered after returning home. While holding the pictures, she describes them as kids who had hopes and dreams and the tragic circumstances of their deaths. One boy was shot by a rival gang while waiting for the school bus in his driveway a few months after returning home. He was 13. At this point in the program, Karen's eyes well up, her voice chokes with sorrow, and her hands tremble. Karen recounts the heartbreaking story of her own son, who was killed by a stranger while selflessly assisting someone he did not know. The sorrow on her face as she recounts the tragedy is palpable. Then she holds up Johnny's obituary photo from the stack, turning it toward the boys. She informs them that Johnny once sat in the room as a mentor but faced drug-related challenges upon going home.

She urges the kids to reflect on what they learned because the men spent time with them from a place of experience and love. The juxtaposition of Johnny's obituary photo with those of the fallen teen boys who likely crossed paths with him before their murders is a disturbing thought. Karen looks around the room and says," 'Never forget what these men went through. Their stories can save you from coming to prison."

Afterward, the boys return to the lobby and prepare to return home, where they likely still encounter gang violence and poverty challenges. The monthly gathering is a testament to the profound selflessness of the JDP men. It is not a magic wand that erases years of social conditioning and environmental influences. It makes no promises of saving every troubled soul who crosses its threshold. But what it does offer is something far more significant—a chance. It provides an opportunity for these boys to witness the firsthand consequences of their actions, immerse themselves in the unforgiving reality of prison life, and learn from compassionate men who once tread the same path as they are heading down. JDP doesn't promise to save every boy who walks through its doors. But it gives them something far more significant—a chance. It's a space where men who have lived through the worst consequences of their actions offer love, wisdom, and hope.

Through JDP, I saw the power of redemption—not just for the boys but for the men who mentor them. It's not perfect. It's not a cure-all. But it's a start. And sometimes, a start is all anyone needs.

LOVE IS THE ONLY FREEDOM

Love is the bridge between you and everything.

Rumi

"Love is an action, never simply a feeling." bell hooks
wrote those words, and I return to them often. Love as action
moves us forward. It transforms and nurtures. I am lucky to
know people who embody this principle. My friend Amy is
one such person.

Amy and I met in 2012 when she contacted me about a
prisoner's submission to my edited volume, *This Side of My
Struggle*. She edited his essay, and I published it. Over the
thirteen years since our initial correspondence, Amy has
become my confidante, a trusted sister in all but name. She

stood beside me during the tumult of my divorce, offering a kindness so steady and brave it felt like a lifeline.

Despite our limited physical time together, Amy has become family, connected by a shared commitment to care deeply, to love without barriers, and to fight for justice.

One of the threads binding us is Keith, a brother whose journey spans more than 25 years in solitary confinement. Keith is a teacher, artist, and relentless social justice scholar. Amy first connected with him through the prisoner whose work I had published. Since then, she and her family have forged a deep, transformative bond with Keith. I, too, love him, though our connection is different—more intellectual and tangential, rooted in the shared purpose of fighting against a broken system.

Keith's story is one of unimaginable endurance. In 1989, after being robbed at gunpoint, he exchanged fire with the perpetrator, one of his childhood friends. Keith was shot twice in the legs. His friend was fatally wounded. Convicted of homicide, Keith received an 18-years-to-life sentence.

While serving his time, Keith was implicated in the infamous 1993 Lucasville prison riot, during which nine prisoners and one guard were killed. Keith has always maintained his innocence, but he was sentenced to death based on a flawed investigation heavily reliant on testimony from prisoners seeking reduced sentences. His memoir, *Condemned*, chronicles his ordeal and the systemic failures of Ohio's criminal justice system.

His story is chronicled in his memoir, Condemned. My joy lies in his profound love for my friend and the countless times he has shown up for my students. Over the past seven to eight years, Keith has been a guest speaker in my classes, discussing the intersections of inequality, race, and poverty.

His unique perspectives and personal experiences spark thought-provoking conversations that challenge our preconceived notions and inspire critical introspection. Keith's immense contributions to my academic work have shed light on the complex social policies within the U.S. criminal justice system. His willingness to engage with the hard questions exemplifies that real people are behind every theory, textbook, and statistical likelihood.

Amy's devotion to Keith's freedom is awe-inspiring. Her list of efforts reads like the résumé of someone who has dedicated their life to a cause. She collaborated with Keith for eight months to bring *Condemned* to life. She traveled to San Francisco, New York City, and Berlin, representing Keith in *The Healing Project* and other events. She facilitated co-teaching opportunities at universities and conferences worldwide and raised funds through auctions of Keith's paintings and merchandise.

Amy established the Native Sons Literacy Project, bringing culturally responsive literature into juvenile detention centers and high schools. She spearheaded the nonprofit *Justice for Keith LaMar,* mediating interviews with figures like Jason Flom of *The Wrongful Conviction Podcast.* She even contributed to Keith's debut album, *Freedom First*, the first album created and released by someone on death row.

The list goes on.

To Amy, though, it isn't a list. It's love in action. She doesn't see her efforts as extraordinary. She simply sees them as necessary.

As much as she pours her heart into supporting Keith, he offers just as much in return. He loves her children as if they were his own and has become a pillar of strength for her family. The love they share is centered on growth and self-improvement—a commitment to becoming the best versions of themselves and inspiring others to do the same. Amy insists the qualities I admire in both her and Keith have emerged from the lessons they have taught each other about authenticity and vulnerability. My perspective on their relationship was limited to phone conversations until I traveled to Ohio and met them in person.

After chatting at her house, Amy and I rode to the prison where Keith is housed. Stepping inside those walls was a moment of reckoning. The conditions were oppressive, and the atmosphere was suffocating. They placed us inside a box-like structure divided by shatterproof glass that simultaneously connected and separated us. Keith was locked in on one side of the box, and Amy and I were sealed in on the other.

They talked, smiled, and shared stories, a kind of symbiotic dance where each movement reflected care, respect, and trust. Watching them, I felt like an interloper, yet they never made me feel like one. Their connection spilled over, wrapping me in its warmth.

Maya Angelou said, "Love has an uncanny knack for recognizing no barriers. It is a fearless force, leaping over hurdles, scaling fences, and penetrating the thickest of walls, always arriving at its destination full of hope." The love between Keith and Amy exemplifies that truth.

§

Over the years, I've stayed connected with Amy and Keith through phone calls, emails, and biweekly Zoom book club meetings. In 2022, eight years after our first meeting, Amy and I reunited during a trip to New York City. She picked up my husband and me, and we spent the evening walking, laughing, and sharing stories over Caribbean food. Keith called briefly during the drive to the airport, his voice a steady reminder of their enduring connection.

Keith and Amy's relationship is not simply about fighting a death sentence, though that fight is at its core. It is about the power of love itself. Love as transformation. Love as resistance. Love as a light that refuses to go out, no matter how dark the night becomes.

§

Keith's execution was initially scheduled for November 16, 2023. The Ohio governor granted him a reprieve, so his execution date has been pushed out to January 13, 2027. Still, a dark cloud hangs ominously. Whispers of prayers and hearts desperately cling to the hope that the date will come and go without incident. But should the state have its way, Amy is committed to being there on that day.

The reservoir of emotional nourishment they have cultivated serves as a sanctuary amid the thorny brambles of their circumstance. Theirs is not an ordinary love story, but it is one of the most profound I have ever witnessed. It reminds me why I continue to care for incarcerated people, despite the toll it sometimes takes on me. In Keith and Amy, I see the best of what love can be: transformative, enduring, and capable of bending even the harshest realities toward something like grace.

And in their light, I am reminded of why I do this work— not for perfection or simplicity, but for the chance to glimpse the extraordinary in the most unexpected places.

IN SEARCH OF MANDELA

It is hard to eulogize any man—to capture in words not just the facts and the dates that make a life, but the essential truth of a person—their private joys and sorrows; the quiet moments and unique qualities that illuminate someone's soul. How much harder to do so for a giant of history, who moved a nation toward justice, and in the process moved billions around the world.

Barack Obama

I fell asleep and almost missed him. My father called, and I knew to turn on the television immediately. News commentators filled the air with words like "legend" and "martyr," marking the gravity of the day. Nelson Mandela was on the verge of freedom after more than 27 years in captivity.

I didn't fully understand Mandela's role as a freedom fighter during my parents' youth, but I was already an ardent supporter of the worldwide divestment efforts against apartheid. His name was everywhere, a rallying cry for justice.

Standing in front of my tiny 13-inch television with its crooked antenna, I wished his jailers would just let him walk free. Tom Brokaw and other reporters droned on, stretching the minutes into an eternity. Finally, the moment came, and Mandela emerged through a haze of smoke—at least, that's how I want to remember it.

Winnie Mandela stood by his side, wearing a proud afro and a smile as radiant as liberation itself. I imagined that same smile would appear on my face decades later when I stood alone, waiting for my husband's release from prison.

The Mandelas held hands, raising their fists in victory. This wasn't just their freedom—it was ours. Alone in my dorm room, I cried my eyeballs out.

§

My friends called in bursts of excitement: "Are? You? Watching? This? Okaybye." "Giiiirrrl, ain't God good? Won't he do it? Alright, call me back."

Frozen on the dorm room floor, I pumped my fist in rhythm with the chants from the crowd. "Freedom! Freedom! Freedom!" The word thundered through the room, through me. Mandela had made the world proud. "Amandla! Amandla!"

You are free now, Baba. The walk seemed heavy on his

hips, and his smile was subdued. The crowd's chants echoed loudly from the back of my TV, and my bellowing barely drowned them out. "Freedom!" I felt all of that. That day, the word *freedom* became indelibly etched in my consciousness. It wasn't just personal anymore. Freedom was power. It was agency, voice, equity, and a fight worth living and dying for.

Years later, I tattooed *freedom* in bold, six-inch-wide letters on my inner arm—a daily reminder of that moment. The day Mandela walked free shifted something in me.

§

Visiting South Africa had been on my bucket list for years, but I had not made it there during Mandela's lifetime. I dreamed of traveling to South Africa for many years. I decided to finalize this book, which I had worked on for over a decade and had completed all but one chapter, the one about my ex-husband. Visiting South Africa lingered on my bucket list for years, though I never made it during Mandela's lifetime. In November 2022, as I approached the end of this memoir, I booked a flight to Cape Town to attend a writing retreat. I had written every chapter except the one about my ex-husband, and it felt fitting to finish the book in Mandela's homeland.

His likeness was everywhere in Cape Town's airport: a beaded statue, photographs, vibrant souvenirs. His face graced every denomination of South African currency, bills I tucked away as keepsakes. Exhausted from 31 hours of travel, I was still energized by the sight of him.

Randall, my driver, noticed my awe and pointed to a panoramic black-and-white photograph of the Mandelas' first walk to freedom in 1990. My chest tightened as memories of that day in my dorm room washed over me.

"Can you snap a photo of me under this?" I handed

Randall my phone, still wrapped in my airplane blanket. Standing beneath the photo, I threw up a fist and smiled, undeterred by the curious stares of passersby.

§

During the ride to my lodge, Randall told me about his children and grandchildren, referring to himself as "colored" because of his multiracial ancestry. I stated that "colored" is an offensive word in the U.S. He knew that, he said. Randall expressed disdain for the lingering effects of apartheid. He pointed to the aluminum shacks in townships piled too close together and explained that they were settlements where many Blacks lived. The poverty was stark.

We drove past an upscale gated estate where the president stays when he is in Cape Town, and Randall's voice expressed disgust when he mentioned massive government corruption. As he pointed to land that was "gifted" by some European dude and a botanical garden founded by some other European dude, I could not help but notice White people everywhere—some driving luxury SUVs alongside us on the highway and others lounging around clear acrylic pools that hung off the sides of condominiums facing the Atlantic Ocean.

During my first three days in Cape Town, the only Black people I saw were service workers, street beggars, and folks standing or sitting on corners waiting for offers of work. The managers at the lodge were an older White couple, and all the cooks and cleaners were Black women and men. I never saw disrespect of any kind, but I noticed how submissive and soft-spoken all the workers were.

The writing coach, Sarah, is a lovely White woman with a South African accent that sounds British to my North American ear. Except for one of the participants and myself, all the participants in the writing retreat were White women, most of whom were born and raised in South Africa. They were all delightful women, and I learned a lot about the role of vulnerability and courage in writing.

Alice, one of the writers, was there to begin a book about her life on Robben Island. Robben Island is an actual island five miles out in the ocean, upon which sits the prison where Nelson Mandela was locked up for most of his 27 years. I had no idea anyone other than prisoners lived there. Alice's husband spent eight years as a correctional officer on Robben Island, and she, along with the other families of jailers, called it home. Alice recalls seeing Mandela whenever he was transported by boat to the hospital for cancer treatment. She lived close enough to see his face and described him as a gentle person whose expressions were dispirited and weary. Alice raised her children on the island. She plans to write a book about the ordinariness of living on an island just footsteps away from where Mandela was incarcerated.

I desperately wanted to see and touch the prison walls on Robben Island, so I booked a tour. Two days later, on the brisk morning of my scheduled tour, I walked to the bottom of the hill from the Victorskloof Lodge to await my driver. I forgot to bring a jacket to Cape Town, so my airplane blanket shrouded my shoulders again. I clutched it as I walked toward what appeared to be a grave marker on the ground near the intersection of a curved street and a deep-inclined brick road with discarded rocks. According to the well-worn gold and black plate marker, "Victoria Road. Built in 1837 with convict labour. Most of the original road has been covered over by recent modern development of this route. An original section of the road remains on the portion known as Victor's Kloof Rd." I had just descended a brick road built by prisoners, most of whom were likely Black. Rarely have I thought about who—literally—paved the road for me to walk on, but this time, I knew. When I arrived at the top, I paid my respects to the imprisoned ancestors of my motherland.

I booked a tour, but on the brisk morning of my scheduled visit, a notification popped up: *canceled.* A taxi strike had paralyzed the city. Disappointed, I asked Miles, my Zimbabwean driver, to take me shopping instead.

At a beachside market, a vendor greeted me with a broad smile. "Where are you from, Sista?"

"The U.S.," I replied.

"Welcome home, Queen." He clasped his hands and offered a slight bow.

The words melted something in me. Standing just yards from the Atlantic Ocean, under the golden warmth of the sun, I felt seen. The moment lingered, buoying me even as I mourned the lost chance to set foot on Robben Island.

I rescheduled the tour for my last day in Cape Town, but fierce winds canceled it again. Staring out at the distant silhouette of Robben Island from the bustling waterfront, I strained to imagine Mandela's life there. Behind me, luxury boutiques buzzed with shoppers.

The juxtaposition stung. I hadn't prepared for the lingering remnants of apartheid to be so stark. The mansions with ocean views. The Black workers toiling quietly. The echoes of systemic inequity.

Amid this renovation, tucked away behind the mall, is a cluster of shops showcasing diamonds and artisanal masterpieces worth a fortune. Only one expansive store sold wares related to African-Black culture. Every cashier was White.

I strained my gaze into the distance, hoping to catch a glimpse of the silhouette of Robben Island. I could barely see it. A profound sense of disappointment washed over me. While I understood that social change takes time, I never expected to encounter such apparent remnants of apartheid nearly thirty years after Nelson Mandela's presidency. Before departing the U.S., I should have watched YouTube videos showcasing modern-day Cape Town. Then I would not have been so shocked by the contrast between multimillion-dollar homes with ocean views and the ubiquity of Black servants scattered throughout the city.

Miles drove me to the airport the next day. As we said our goodbyes, he shared his dream of visiting the U.S.

"It's not easy for us. We need sponsors, visas, proof of funds—everything."

"I'll sponsor you," I said impulsively.

His face lit up. "What? You will?"

"Sure," I said. "You do what you need on this side. You can stay with me when you arrive. I'll help you find work."

As my plane lifted off, I reflected on my time in South Africa. Though I never set foot on Robben Island, I carried its lessons with me. Freedom is not static; it's a living, breathing struggle. It requires vigilance, justice, and humanity.

That's what Mandela believed. That's what his life taught me. And that's what I will always carry forward.

LOSING THE FIRST 200 POUNDS IS THE HARDEST

I don't need you. I never needed you.

Text message, Xavier, June 2019

I held onto LaMichael tightly while riding on the back of his motorcycle. Just as in our everyday lives, I leaned into him, and he kept me safe. The roar of his Honda Shadow soothed me. My arms clung to his torso as I rested my helmeted cheek against his broad back. With my eyes gently shut, I exhaled into the kind of peace that comes when you know you're protected. The traffic light changed, and LaMichael zoomed forward in a burst. As we rounded the corner, he leaned. I leaned. But then, I opened my eyes—and there he was. My ex-husband. Perched on his Harley, his booted foot planted as though he were anchoring the weight of his body and that noisy, overcompensating machine he couldn't afford. Without a thought, I gave him the middle finger.

I hope that motherfucker saw me.

§

Our story began a few years earlier, in December 2014. Xavier was incarcerated on a 25-to-life sentence. I met him during a volunteer visit when I spoke to a group of protective custody prisoners, including former cops, sex offenders, elderly and disabled men, trans women, and gang dropouts. Xavier was at that prison because he turned state's witness and testified against a murderer whose boots he wore on the night the man killed his elderly godparents for drug money. He and Xavier had been neighbors at a cheap motel. The murderer and his girlfriend were in one room, and Xavier sat next door, smoking crack, and drowning in pornography, and hiding out between robberies. Prior to this term, he had only been in the free world for a month after serving six years of a 12-year sentence for the same crime. By the time we met, he had turned his life around and become a model prisoner.

Karen, the JDP mentor I'd come to adore, invited me to speak. I was delighted with the opportunity. I arrived to find about forty men seated in a circle, their standard blue prison uniforms blending into the dull surroundings. The hum of their chatter fell silent when I walked in.

Xavier rushed to greet me with an eager grin, his hairless face shining with excitement. He carried a stack of papers—my bio, printed and highlighted. "Please don't pass that around," I said gently, forcing a smile. Despite saying he was fine with it, he seemed disappointed.

I brought colorful laminated strips of paper with

encouraging quotes for each participant. After introducing ourselves, the prisoners went around the room, reading the passages aloud and sharing how their lives were reflected in the quotes. As they talked about aspiring to be closer to their children or regretting their choices, I offered words of support to each of them.

Xavier's contribution stood out. "I'm holding space," he said, his voice measured, his expression sincere. I'd never heard the phrase before, but it intrigued me enough that I Googled it later that night. *Holding space* is the act of creating an environment for others to feel seen, heard, and respected. It's about offering presence without judgment, withholding advice, and honoring someone's journey.

I loved that.

A transgender woman shared her pain over a family that refused to accept her. Once a gang shot caller in Los Angeles, she now wrestled with showing her mother the same respect her mother had denied her. My voice caught fire. "Don't compromise yourself," I told her, my words pouring out like a sermon. "Authenticity is all you owe anybody." I went on for five minutes, but the truth is, I wasn't just talking to her—I was exorcising my own demons.

The group was a kaleidoscope of humanity—different races, ages, crimes, and life stories converging in that room. I met each man's vulnerability with my own compassion. Whether it was the old white man who'd murdered his wife or the young gang member who burned down a house, I didn't flinch. For the lifers without the possibility of parole, hope is rare. I offered it freely, knowing the weight of my words might be all they'd carry out of that room.

The quick 75 minutes passed quickly. As I wrapped up, Xavier quietly moved to the back of the room while a line of men formed in front of me, each waiting to shake my hand. One inmate, nicknamed Frog for his bulging eyes, interrupted the flow. "Damn, Girl. You blew my wig back."

I wasn't sure what that meant, but I decided to take it as a compliment. Since that day, I've considered myself capable of blowing wigs back.

In the parking lot, Karen and I debriefed. We spoke about the men, the energy in the room, and, inevitably, Xavier. Xavier, she said, was a star—a model of rehabilitation and potential. Her admiration for the man was palpable, and it planted a seed in me.

She believed it was a shame that he was still in prison. He felt disappointed that, aside from a couple of people, Xavier had little support outside of the prison. Although his mom accepted his phone calls and sent him quarterly packages, Karen expressed disappointment that she hadn't visited Xavier in umpteen years. She lived about eight hours away. His aunt and cousin lived nearby and visited him regularly. His father died of AIDS when Xavier was a boy, and he did not have many other people outside of the prison supporting him.

Karen raved about how far Xavier had come, how well-trusted he was, and how he had thrived since being at the prison. People adored him and were impressed with his ability to help other men maintain sobriety. Her adoration caught my ear. "Would it be alright if I wrote to him?" I asked, almost surprising myself. She smiled knowingly, sure we'd hit it off.

§

For months, Xavier and I exchanged letters. He was a beautiful writer—thoughtful, articulate, and vulnerable. The depth in his words pulled me closer, and before long, our connection spilled over into phone calls. By then, he was gently nudging Karen to involve me in more events at the prison.

Several months later, Xavier nudged Karen to ask me and a few other volunteers to assist with a fundraising event at the prison. Our task would be to count the number of laps prisoners ran, and sponsors would pay by the lap or mile. Xavier, ever the overachiever, ran 23 laps—just shy of eight miles. Running wasn't a hobby for him; it was a lifeline. His feet hit the pavement every day, rain or shine, a rhythmic ritual that kept him centered. Sometimes he was late calling because the prison's movement stifled his ability to get outside on time; he always mentioned the number of laps or hours he'd gotten in by the time he reached me. Apart from running, Xavier also facilitated various groups, like the one where I first encountered him. By the time we met, he had already earned a couple of associate's degrees and was taking classes to eventually earn a bachelor of arts degree. He was a star.

And, as I had done previously, I caught feelings.

Falling for a prisoner defies simple explanation. In my case, it was not just one thing but a combination of factors that drew me in. I love words, and he used lots of them to make me feel special. Incarcerated women and men often crave and provide affection unreservedly, and the emotional expressions can be intense. What mattered to me the most was not whether someone was free or incarcerated but their ability to be present, share laughter, provide support, and show kindness during every challenge. So, I waited breathlessly in anticipation of letters and phone calls. We even discussed my possibly visiting him, but it meant I could no longer volunteer at the prison. Ultimately, I decided to make the sacrifice.

When I saw Xavier again, six months after that first meeting, he looked the same but felt different. Our letters and calls had bridged a chasm. By then, I was driving down to see him almost every weekend. At first, I stayed in hotels, but the costs piled up, so I found Airbnb's—and even spent two consecutive Christmases with a sweet, elderly white woman who treated me like family.

Xavier and I got along well, and he enjoyed listening to me talk about one of my favorite pastimes, thrift store shopping. I shared about all the discarded items at thrift stores that were given a second chance at life, things that were popular back when he was on the streets, like George Foreman grills and CD players. I learned a lot about him, too. He liked to read more than watch TV and was a good writer. Because of his involvement in the dog training program, he had a cell to himself and took turns with his friend Paul for overnight stays with the dog.

§

Every prison visiting room has its own heartbeat—a symphony of tears, laughter, and stolen moments. The desperation is thick, but so is the connection. Families and lovers pour in from miles away, each clutching their own reasons for enduring the razor wire and walls. I enjoyed being part of a community because, aside from the families and lovers who drove for hours every weekend and stood in line together, no one else seemed to understand what inspired me to accept a relationship with a prisoner.

Xavier affectionately referred to me as "the mayor" due to my outgoing and sociable nature. I greeted other visitors with hugs and was always eager to hear updates about paroles and appeals. I make friends quite easily.

One woman, whom Xavier and I called "Imelda Marcos," was impeccably dressed every weekend. She always arrived early, dressed to the nines in faux fur, flashy jewelry, and chunky high-heeled shoes. Sometimes, Imelda wore enormous hats with a tilt so deep we could only see one of her eyes. Other times, she wore a clipped flower in her shiny black hair. Despite standing barely five feet tall, her smile was humongous. I once told her she was the sweetest person among us, even on the busiest days.

Imelda's husband is the stepfather of her adult children. Her elementary school-aged granddaughters told a nurse that he touched their nipples and "down there." Finding the accusations unbelievable, Imelda abandoned her home and family ten hours away and moved closer to her incarcerated husband. They were relegated to the "sex offenders" section of the room each week, seats farthest from the toys and TV. They will never be allowed a conjugal visit due to the nature of her husband's crimes. Obviously, I did not have the same challenges as Imelda, but I still wondered what kept her so passionately committed despite the chaos he caused in her life. How did the two maintain a tight connection? What strategies did Imelda use to prevent herself from sinking into despair?

Rita, another lovely person I befriended, was someone I saw frequently on weekends. She is a devoted wife, and she and Mike are drama-free. We had coffee at the mall after our visit once, and she was cheerful and in love. Rita had been riding through this bid with Mike since the late '90s. Xavier had nothing but praise for Mike, who has an LWOP sentence, meaning Rita has to ride with him a lot longer. That was not going to be Xavier and me, I told myself. His ass was going home—come hell or high water. Mike and Rita were afforded weekend visits every few months, which likely helped maintain constancy and stamina in their marriage. Could there be the magic of having 72 hours of alone time? If so, I wanted that, too.

I was also friendly with Evelyn, a stunning church wife who always rocked gorgeous dresses and crystal-encrusted stilettos. Evelyn and the pastor prayed unabashedly, holding hands and speaking in tongues at the start and end of every visit. A church pastor at the time of his arrest he had sexually assaulted a young boy in a public restroom. The charges, for which the pastor still maintains his innocence, paint him as a predator with repeated assaults on young men and boys. Xavier said the pastor was gay and pointed to his boyfriend, who occasionally visited with a woman halfway across the room. The pastor is effeminate, so I imagine Evelyn was aware of the possibility that he was bisexual or gay. She remained devoted for the long term, possibly because of their powerful faith connection and satisfaction as spiritual companions. They, too, would never have conjugal visits. Evelyn typically arrived later than most partners, so I never spent time with her enough to ask how she maintained her unconditional love for him. I hoped I had found my person, too.

Cynthia and Paul were also a sweet couple. Paul had been locked up for over 35 years and was one of Xavier's closest friends. Cynthia and Paul married on the patio of the visiting room and were allowed conjugal visits soon after. We had a few phone conversations after they were married to discuss how things were going. I yearned for a weekend stay with Xavier, so I asked her about the privacy of the cabins, wondering if that was the factor that kept them so close. She was on cloud nine, but Xavier said a relationship with

Cynthia was just something for Paul to do until he was released because he believed the two were incompatible.

Another person I liked was Carol, a 49-year-old executive who fell for her 23-year-old former intern. She and I developed a friendship and began having dinner and drinks after our visits ended. I told her how pretty she was every time I saw her. She is stunning, with smooth and flawless skin and a captivating smile. Week after week, she dazzled with stylish wedge heels, blingy t-shirts, and confidence. She and I started chatting while in line at the vending machines and as we walked down the hill toward our cars when the visits ended. Once, I asked her if she wanted to have dinner and drinks at the Cheesecake Factory. Thus began a lovely friendship over appetizers, pink drinks, and warm dark rolls.

Carol's dude always entered the visiting room with a swagger. They looked at each other lovingly, and she lit up whenever she saw him. Xavier said he was not doing much with his life besides hanging around gang bangers on the yard. He was in prison for robbing someone and had received a gang enhancement, meaning more time to serve, because he used the victim's cellphone to record himself throwing up gang signs.

His knucklehead ass would eventually cheat on Carol by having another woman visit him. One Saturday, I was seated with Xavier when we saw him kissing, rubbing on, and giggling all day with a woman who was not Carol. Xavier warned me not to say anything to Carol because he did not want Knucklehead to start any shit with him. But she had already texted me by the time I arrived at my car, asking if I knew why he rejected her visit. Carol and I had become friends, and I was not about to keep his ugly secret from her.

"Girl, it's 'because he had another woman in there with

him today." Watching that unfold was a mess. She deserved so much better, and she knew she did. She softened slightly with his apology, but she never bounced back. Not long after his triflin' ass was with that other woman, who Knucklehead learned also had a dude at San Quentin, Carol walked away and never looked back. She and I connected so well, perhaps because we shared the experience of being successful Black women who fell in love with men who had nothing to offer us except love. Sometimes, love is enough.

Until it's not.

§

Xavier gave me the tea on everybody. "He can't out-think his dick" was how many of our gossip sessions began. "That guy? Caught in the shower with a trans woman." "That one over there? Jerked off in front of the female officers." "This one? Creeping with an employee." Everyone had a story, and Xavier served them up piping hot. I leaned in for the juice like it was the antidote to prison grayness.

For two years, we circled that same drab patio, hand in hand, laughing, gossiping, dreaming. Once around. Then again. And again. Always in the same direction—no reversing, no mingling with other inmates, no stepping too fast lest it look like running. We strolled deliberately, noticing the cracks in the cement where lizards darted in and out. I once pointed to the parking lot beyond the fence, and we riffed about how someday, we'd drive away together in my Camaro. I'm sure we walked dozens of miles around that patio, imagining a future painted brighter than the institutional gray that surrounded us.

Xavier wasn't my type physically, but our conversations were a gravitational pull I couldn't resist. He made me think, made me laugh, made me feel seen. Attraction grew in the spaces between our words, building on respect and understanding. I didn't need his looks to light me up. His mind and his spirit did the job.

§

Sitting in my car, I was on the phone with Xavier one day outside a convenience store. A White guy backed in next to me, but too close. "Please don't hit my car," I said, knowing he heard me because both windows were down. Then he opened his car door, hit my driver's side door, and walked toward the store.

"What the fuck? At least apologize, asshole."

He turned, met my gaze, and spat out the word: "Monkey."

My blood boiled. I jumped out of my car, phone still clutched to my ear, Xavier's voice a distant hum. "You racist motherfucka!" I yelled, taking a few steps toward him. His Latina girlfriend emerged from the passenger seat, screaming, "He is not a racist!" I wanted her to shut up.

"Fuck this bitch. Let's go." He opened the driver's side door and got in his car.

"Fuck both of y'all!" I was hot. My hands shook as I grabbed the steering wheel and backed out.

Due to time constraints, my call with Xavier was abruptly cut off. Xavier immediately called his mom and told her to check on me. She phoned me as soon as I got back in my car and advised me that it's not wise to teeter between being right and dead right. True.

As Xavier and I circled the patio the following weekend, he admonished me: "You can't just argue with people you don't know. When I get home, I'mma dig in that ass if you do that again." That was the first time he made me feel unsafe. Something about his words made my stomach knot. He stood a little taller, his voice edged with something I hadn't heard before. I didn't like how it felt. Instead of asking him to clarify, I defended my anger at the man who'd disrespected me. Later, I wished I'd spoken up about how his comment landed. For days, it gnawed at me, but I convinced myself he hadn't meant any harm.

A few days later, I told my department chair about him during one of our cardio walks. I raved about Xavier—his brilliance, his growth, his resilience. Then, almost as an afterthought, I mentioned what he'd said.

She stopped mid-stride. "He said what, Nandi? Umph. I don't like that."

"I didn't like it either, Sara," I admitted, "but I don't think he meant it badly."

Her raised eyebrows said everything I was trying to deny.

That evening, I wrote Xavier a letter, pouring out my frustration. The next time we spoke, he apologized immediately. His tone was serious, reflective. "I get why you felt that way. I didn't think before I said it, but I see now. I'm sorry. It won't happen again."

§

Xavier's associate's degree graduation ceremony at the prison was scheduled for a Thursday at 10 a.m. I visited him the weekend prior and asked him multiple times if he wanted me to attend. Each time, he said no. Considering I had to teach in the afternoon, he expressed concern about me traveling extensively before work. Then, on Wednesday, the night before the ceremony, he called and said he wanted me to come. I didn't want to go. But I went. Because that's who I was with him: the cheerleader, the one who showed up.

Xavier wanted me there because he craved validation

like oxygen. I'd seen it in his eyes the first day we met, when I stopped him from passing around those printed bios of me. He wanted people to see him as he was now, not who he'd been in the chaos of his addiction. He carried his accomplishments like armor against the shame that clung to him. And prison—by design—rips at your self-worth until you're raw. So, I drove the four-plus hours round trip, even when it drained me, because he needed it. And because I loved him.

§

While on another patio walk, we rotated left in the area adjacent to the conjugal visit cabins. I said, "One of these days, I'm going to marry you."

He agreed. Just like that, we were engaged.

I had never been married, but Xavier had. He cheated on his wife, who eventually served him divorce papers while he was in prison. He said he was no longer the person who cheated, and I believed him. I didn't know what else had gone awry in their marriage, but I trusted that he was not that same man.

Initially, we didn't set a date due to the lengthy application process, which involved gathering my birth certificate, a marriage license, notaries on both ends and administrative approval from the prison. Once they have all the documents and permissions, someone at the facility shares the next available date on their calendar. I also had to purchase a wedding band and send it to the prison with its receipt. Other partners told me I should get the paperwork going as soon as possible because the process takes months. I was eager to take my relationship with my fiancé to the next level and be able to spend time alone getting to know him.

The court filing had to be done in the same county as the prison, and since the courthouse is about 40 miles past the prison, I made the trek once the official told us we could get a date on the calendar. I arrived, filed the paperwork, and met the man authorized to officiate prison ceremonies.

He was covered in tattoos and had a long gray beard adorning his weathered face. He was far from the wedding officiant I imagined when I pictured my dream wedding. His hair was tied back in a stringy ponytail that reached down his back. The overall effect reminded me of a curious fusion between a character from Duck Dynasty and someone recently released from serving a long stint in prison. After discussing the details, he requested $225 to cover his fees. We agreed he would arrive between 10 and 10:30 a.m. Before leaving the courthouse lobby, I took a moment to ensure he knew how to pronounce my name correctly.

"It's Nandi, like Gandhi. Please don't say it as if it rhymes with candy. It's important that you pronounce it correctly at my wedding."

"Naaahndi. I got it." He folded my check and headed toward the parking lot.

Speaking of names, I talked to Xavier about hyphenating our surnames. We would both have new last names once we were married. Despite his lack of enthusiasm, he agreed.

§

My mother and I exchanged the following text the night before the wedding, just hours before my friends arrived at my house for a pre-wedding celebration.

Me: Ma, the other day when I told you about my wedding, you said, 'I wish you wouldn't.' How come you said that?

Ma: Because I always pray and ask God for blessings for you. You are soooo much more deserving of a better life than that one.

Me: That makes me very sad. My life will be extraordinary, Ma.

I spent the afternoon heartbroken that I did not have my mother's support. She feared another nadir fiasco. But she did not know Xavier, so I understood. My mother's well-meaning concerns felt like a shroud cast over my celebration, and I had to pull myself together as my guests began trickling in. The dissonance between her perception and my dreams gnawed at the joy I should have been feeling on the eve of my wedding. It was a moment of deep emotional struggle.

I invited my friends over for a pre-wedding party. I put on a happy face to match my cute T-shirt that read: ~~GIRLFRIEND~~. ~~FIANCÉ~~. WIFE. I felt a mix of emotions. On the one hand, I was overjoyed to be marrying the man I loved. But on the other hand, I could not shake the feeling that my wedding would not be what I had always imagined for myself. I had pictured a jubilant ceremony with all my loved ones gathered around, not a makeshift affair on a prison patio. But even with all the imperfections and shortcomings, I knew my love for Xavier was genuine. And in the end, that was all that truly mattered.

During the party, Xavier called. I connected my phone to the stereo so his voice could blast across the room. Everyone wanted to congratulate him, too. One of my friends, Darlene, who had spent more than 20 years in prison, was eager to tell him she understood precisely what he was feeling. She spoke directly into the stereo output speaker amid chuckles around the room and told him twice that he was lucky to have me.

Before the celebration ended, I asked each person to write tips for a successful lifetime marriage. The overwhelming suggestion was the virtue of communication. No one else echoed my aunt Shelia's advice the night before, hinting at a more pragmatic, less romantic approach to marital bliss: hang in there as long as the pros outweigh the cons. I whispered a silent prayer to the universe that the scale of our marital happiness would always tip in favor of the pros and that the cons would never gain enough weight to shatter us. I did not have another heartbreak in me, and I told Xavier that multiple times.

After consulting a few of my closest friends to learn my favorite flavor, my dear friend Kimberlee brought out a gourmet cake she had specially ordered. Red velvet. She nudged me to cut a slice to save in the freezer for our first anniversary. I carved a massive piece around our names, wrapped it in foil, and placed the sweet goodness in the freezer.

Multiple times during the party, people asked when he'd be home. "No idea," I said on repeat. "No idea."

Before going to bed, I laid out my outfit. Per Xavier's suggestion, I purchased and planned to wear a t-shirt that read, "Got one!" The stick figures pictured on the shirt were a bride dragging an (ostensibly) unwilling husband. I told him I saw that and other cute ones. We agreed that one was funny, so he nudged me to buy it.

I ironed my floor-length purple African wax print skirt, carefully tending to every crease and fold to ensure it looked pristine. My 3-inch brown retro clogs kept my skirt a few inches from touching the ground, so I was sure to polish and set them aside. I pulled out my go-to hair gel, Miss Jessie's Pillow Soft Curls. As the night gradually turned into the morning, I was still awake.

I wore sweatpants, sneakers, and my wedding tee during the drive. On the last stretch of highway, before reaching the prison, I stopped at a gas station and grabbed my skirt, which had been flung over the passenger seat. I walked towards the bathroom in the convenience store, placing my skirt over the toilet paper holder on the wall. I stepped carefully around the water leaking from the back of the toilet while I rummaged through my cosmetic bag for lip rouge, gold eyeshadow, and edge control gel. I checked how fine I looked in the piece of mirror that hung on the wall, brushed my teeth to erase the coffee smell, and sniffed under my arms to ensure my lavender and frankincense mixture was still potent. Although it was early in the morning, it was mid-July. My hot flashes could have made me funky before noon.

When I reached the entrance of the prison parking lot, I told Officer Hernandez in the booth that it was my wedding day. He smiled and congratulated me, though he might have been thinking the same thing I would have thought if I were still in uniform. "Don't do it. You don't know that man."

As I stood in the check-in line, I added $100 to my vending machine card and purchased 10 tokens for photographs. I was thrilled to share my news with everyone in line—I am getting married!

Xavier's best man, Paul, walked through the big door with him. Paul said Xavier was about to come out in a wrinkled shirt, and he stopped him and got his boy right. Moments later, Mark, a second friend, came through the door. Mark's wife regularly visited, but she kept to herself. She did not know about his sexual relationship with a transgender prisoner. Xavier jokingly said the trans woman was their Yoko Ono, referring to her infamous role in splitting up the Beatles.

I told Paul and Mark they could choose whatever they wanted from the vending machines. Paul's wife, Xavier's aunt, cousin, and cousin-in-law soon joined us right before the officiant arrived. I reminded him how important it was to pronounce my name correctly. "It's Naaaaaahndi," I said as I made a loop with my lips to accentuate the aaaaaaah sound that I hoped he'd make.

With a dismissive gesture, he said, "I remember."

Not ten minutes later, during the part of the ceremony where one traditionally says, "Do you take—?" he made a sound that came out of his as "Nandy." I turned toward him and rolled my eyes. Xavier looked at me with a subdued chuckle, as I had already told him that this dude better pronounce my name right, or I would request a refund.

Xavier and I held hands during the entire ceremony; he squeezed my fingers and sweated. I had never seen him so nervous before. At the end, the guy said, "Xavier and Nandy, I now pronounce you—."

"Nahndi. It's Naaaaaaaahndi," I erupted. My annoyance was evident before we shared a too-wet kiss. I then bellowed, "I'se married now," loud enough for members of our small party to check for onlookers. Indeed, there were. A couple circled the patio in our background, holding hands just as we had and would continue to do for another year, month, week, and day.

We took group photos and then a few of just Xavier and me. I attempted to persuade the photographer to snap a picture of us locking lips or with me sitting on his lap. However, an officer had to approve all photos, and the inmate photographer risked getting into trouble for breaking the rules. He politely declined. After the pictures, my wedding party and I played a game of UNO for about an hour. Whenever Xavier hit me with a reverse card or made me draw four, he burst into hearty laughter.

"Sorry, Wife," he said while I looked at him sideways.

His friends returned to the housing area at about noon, and his family departed a bit after 1 p.m.

Evelyn and the pastor were supposed to sing at the wedding, but they came late. She was stuck in traffic and arrived after Mr. I-Pronounce-You-and-Mispronounce-Your-Name had already departed. While waiting for the pastor to come through the big door, she asked me to tell him there was traffic on the freeway. Even after I told him there was, he stayed frustrated with her for a while. The two sang a duet to us on the patio later in the day, and it was beautiful.

A few minutes before 3 o'clock, the officer announced that the visiting room was closing, which was our cue to hold our bodies close for a few seconds. Again, we shared a too-wet kiss.

I said, "Bye, Husband."

"Bye, Wife," he responded.

On the way out of the prison, I used the bottleneck of the checkout line to tell everyone I had just gotten married. A few women mentioned that they were waiting for the paperwork process to make its way up the chain so it could be their turn. Another woman told me she had just gotten married the week before and could not wait for her family visit, which most people know as a conjugal visit, so she could truly get to know her husband.

I walked to my car at the bottom of the hill, stepping slowly because the clogs and long skirt combo felt more burdensome than they had in the morning when I felt fancy—despite getting dressed in a convenience store bathroom. As soon as I sat in my car, I used my cell phone to snap photos of the pictures we took, and I sent them to my closest friends, family, and new mother-in-law.

I drove to the Cheesecake Factory and waited two hours for Xavier's family. Between three fruity martinis and a lot of free bread, I stared lovingly at our photos and played Candy Crush on my phone. I was happy to be married but sad that I was alone. I inched my way out of the gloom— albeit not so swiftly because of the fruity martinis.

When his aunt and cousins arrived, they welcomed me into the family. We ate and then went our separate ways. I headed to my Airbnb and waited for Xavier's phone call. Per prison policy, we had only 15 minutes to gush about our marriage before being disconnected. The following day was Sunday, so I woke up and returned to prison for a second visit.

§

Three months later, when the dust of our wedding had settled, I decided it was time to introduce my mother to my husband. Her flight arrived from Baltimore at about 10 p.m. on a Friday, and I drove to a hotel near the prison so we could arrive at the facility early.

He was bubbly and tried hard to impress her. He kept swiveling toward her for long periods, so his back was to me, and his right buttock hung partially off his chair. I tapped him on the shoulder three times throughout the morning and asked him why I was staring entirely at the back of his head. He apologized the first two times, adjusted his body to include me, and then seemed annoyed when I called him out the third time. I chalked it up to his deep desire to impress my mom, but I was bothered, and he was beginning to grate on my nerves. When 1 o'clock rolled around, I said I was ready to leave.

I wish I had a time machine, and my mother had had the vision to say the following profound words before we exited:

If one day you ever have a change of heart and decide that you don't love my daughter anymore, please don't hurt her. Just bring her back to me.

In the viral video where I first heard those words, a teary-eyed father said them to his future son-in-law. My mother wanted nothing more than for me to be happy, and Xavier's eagerness to impress her that day convinced her he was committed.

§

Xavier and I were granted the privilege of conjugal visits every few months—72 uninterrupted hours together in a modest cabin on the prison grounds. Check-in was always the same: standing in the lobby while an officer meticulously inspected every item in my clear plastic bag. They sifted through my underwear, scrutinized the papers accompanying my medication, turned every pocket inside out, and unscrewed the caps from my toothpaste, lotion, lube, and body wash. I understood the need for caution, but it didn't make the process any less intrusive.

Only three prisoners at a time were allowed conjugal visits, simply because only three cabins were in usable condition. The waiting room always had wives and, sometimes, small children. After we cleared the inspection, an officer escorted us to the cabins, where we waited—sometimes for two hours—for our loved ones to arrive.

The cabins, built in the 1980s, were tiring but serviceable. Each had two small bedrooms, a kitchen, a living room, and a bathroom. The refrigerator came pre-stocked with $250 worth of food I ordered in advance—cereal, frozen fries, soda, fruit, chicken wings, pizza, oatmeal, and the essentials: condiments, bread, milk, chips, and coffee. Still, roaches were a constant battle, so I cleaned the place from top to bottom as I waited for Xavier. The donated sheets had long lost their elastic, clinging loosely to cracked, vinyl-covered mattresses that had likely been there since the '80s. A worn DVD player and TV sat in the living room. Olive and avocado-green floors added a dated charm, and the small patio outside offered a sliver of freedom—a place to watch the birds or lose ourselves in the night sky. The cabin smelled stale and hollow, but it was our home for those weekends, and despite the guards' regular calls for Xavier to step outside and be counted, we were grateful for that privacy.

I remember our first argument during one of those weekends. Xavier said something that cut deeper than I expected, and I wanted one of his familiar, soft apologies. Instead, he asked, flatly, if my tears were necessary. I retreated to the second bedroom, sobbing into the stale air. I found a discarded crossword puzzle book and began scribbling thoughts as if they could anchor me. Twice, Xavier cracked the door open and asked if we could just move past it. I stared at the walls and wondered if this was what marriage was supposed to feel like. I didn't feel safe—not in the way that mattered. Safety is trust, encouragement, accountability, and validation—all the things I gave him freely. Safety is knowing you can express yourself without judgment or fear of being dismissed. That was the space he promised to hold for me, and yet, in that moment, it felt hollow.

His patience for my sadness was thin that day. His past

apologies had felt sincere, but now, it seemed like I was just irritating him. It was the first time I saw how he struggled with vulnerability—his and mine. His annoyance clung to the air, making me second-guess my feelings. I tore up the note I had written to myself—a failed attempt to self-soothe. I told myself things would be better once he was free. But deep down, I wondered: would he always retreat into silence when I needed words? Would he offer empty space when I needed comfort? Would he choose coldness when kindness was called for?

The next morning, when the officer arrived to check us out, Xavier and I exchanged a small hug and a fleeting kiss. Tears burned down my cheeks as I joined the other women at the gate.

When I got home, I sat at my computer and reread old letters I had written to him. In one, I had typed:

"I reread some of your blog entries. I must have blocked it out or forgotten, but I didn't realize you were a three-striker. I'm sure you told me. My heart felt heavy, like I was hearing it for the first time. I didn't know you had been incarcerated twice before. You also mentioned spending your youth chasing approval from others. You struggled with self-worth. Can you pinpoint when that started? We all want to belong, especially when we're young. I'm just curious where that came from."

Xavier often blamed his stunted emotional growth and drug use on his mother's remarriage. She had been a teenage mom who spoiled him endlessly, but everything shifted when she married. He felt pushed aside, no longer the center of her world. The constant tension between Xavier and his stepfather became a breeding ground for rebellion, driving him to seek attention elsewhere—to feel alive or numb, whichever came first.

His mother was fierce, unafraid to bare her vulnerabilities. But that raw honesty terrified him. He loved her, but he couldn't be authentic with her. When honesty felt too risky, he'd ask me to speak for him. But I barely knew his mother—how could I mediate that? I kept our interactions polite, though her presence lingered like an unspoken question.

Xavier's irritation with her ran deep. She had refinanced her home in his name, thinking it would secure his future if something happened to her. But he saw it as proof she never believed he'd be free. He resented her for it. He told me— twice—that once he got the house out of his name, he'd cut her off completely. His willingness to discard her should have been a warning. It was the canary in the coal mine I chose to ignore.

§

Men began filtering in at 8:55 a.m., each striding toward waiting arms—children squealing, women embracing, parents holding back tears. But Xavier didn't come. By 9:25, frustration prickled under my skin. At 9:30, I asked the officer if Xavier had been notified. He assured me everyone had been called. I sat back down, watching other families reunite, feeling increasingly invisible.

At 10:00, I asked again. My anger simmered—was it understaffing or just cruelty? I blamed the system, the guards, even some faceless prisoner causing a lockdown. Then a lanky white guy I recognized walked by.

"Xavier will be out soon. He just finished running the track and went to shower."

"He was out running?" My voice sharpened. My mood soured.

When Xavier finally appeared, sweaty and bouncing, I asked why he was late.

"I had to wait for a shower."

"Lanky Guy said you were outside running the track."

He scowled. "That motherfucker talks too much."

By then, my excitement had cooled. It took me an hour to shake the mood. Xavier kept grumbling about Lanky Guy, but I couldn't stop wondering—would he always choose his own needs first? I knew running kept him sober, but it felt like another addiction—one he prioritized over me.

§

We got in line when the afternoon re-up of the vending machines happened. We flirted a bit and chatted with the other couples. As we were returning to our table, he said thank you.

"That's new," I commented, not sounding as snarky as it might seem.

"What do you mean?" He had no idea.

"You have never thanked me for the food I bought you. That was the first time." Imelda overheard our conversation, and her brow furrowed.

"No, it's not." He was unsure whether it was or not.

I had thought about it for over a year and was keenly aware that he never once thanked me for the overpriced snacks, sandwiches, and drinks I bought from the machines. Without fail, he always entered the visiting room to a table full of Sour Patch Kids, soda, hot wings, and other items he enjoyed. The machines were empty well before midday, and he and I jumped in line for more candy, chips, sandwiches, and soda when they were replenished. He gushed over the food for a year, remarked how delicious everything was compared to prison food, and woofed it down gleefully. Never once had he said thank you.

"I'm sorry. Thank you." He later said he was disappointed in himself that he had taken so long to show his appreciation and would do better. It was my own fault for not saying something. I guess.

§

Speaking of generosity, I contacted officials about a "recall of sentence," which he had been advised would be his best bet for getting out of prison. After submitting the application and waiting a few months, I received the following email:

Parole Hearings has thus far declined to exercise its authority under Penal Code Section 1170(d) to refer matters to the court for a recall of sentence. Another avenue that Xavier may wish to pursue is a commutation of his sentence by the governor. Information about this process can be found on the governor's website.

Goddamnit.

Determined, I immediately emailed Scott Kernan, the head of the California Department of Corrections and Rehabilitation, asking for advice. His assistant responded, explaining that Xavier's indeterminate sentence—minimum 25 years with a life maximum—meant he didn't qualify for recall. A governor's commutation was his only option. The clock reset, and we jumped into action.

Xavier filled out the application, and I kept the process moving. The bureaucratic hurdles were maddening. Calls and letters from prisoners often go unanswered, leaving advocates like me to shoulder the legwork. I spent hours navigating red tape, making calls, and sending emails. Once, I used my professional title and university email to contact a high-ranking official, which backfired. The official notified the university president, who then contacted my dean. The reprimand I received was stern, and the message clear: use university resources again, and I'd face consequences.

Undeterred, I contacted all five junior colleges Xavier had attended to request his transcripts and have them forwarded to my university. My plan was to secure his college admission before his commutation review as proof of his readiness to thrive outside prison. At first, his application was denied because he hadn't met one general education requirement.

This setback didn't stop me. Armed with a triple latte, I met with the Director of Admissions over lunch, shared our story, and appealed to her heart. She agreed to grant him conditional admission if he promised to complete the missing class immediately after release. I paid his tuition, added the acceptance letter to his commutation packet, and applied for a $5,000 scholarship on his behalf. When he was selected to receive it, I was ecstatic. I had to decline because he wasn't released in time.

§

The commutation hearing with the Board of Parole finally arrived. Though Xavier couldn't leave the prison to attend, he was allowed to have people speak on his behalf. Early that morning, I drove to a government building in downtown Sacramento. Most inmates had no advocates present. Travel costs and the five-minute speaking limit likely deterred many. Xavier's aunt, cousin, and Karen were there with me.

Karen spoke first, offering a glowing testament to Xavier's character. She described him as a model inmate: educated, sober, and dedicated to helping others. Her calm measured delivery set the tone. Then it was my turn.

I approached the podium.

"My name is Dr. Nandi Sojourner Crosby. I chair the Department of Sociology at California State University, Chico. Xavier is my husband. We're two mature individuals who've built a strong relationship through letters, phone calls, visits, and overnight stays. He will come home to a community of educated, law-abiding individuals ready to mentor, support, and befriend him. He's been accepted into college, and I will ensure he has the resources to thrive. Xavier deserves a second chance."

One Board member asked pointedly, "What do you think about the fact that prison relationships often don't survive once someone is released?"

I didn't flinch. "Sir, I'm confident we'll beat the odds. We're almost 50. Even if we don't last as husband and wife, we'll always be friends."

When it ended, I checked the website at 3 p.m. The news hit like fireworks—his commutation was approved. My fingers flew across my phone. "He's coming home!" I screamed into one call after another, as though Mandela himself had been freed. I called everyone: my mama, his mama, my closest friends, my aunt. I couldn't stop smiling.

When I reached the warden's office, I asked them to connect me with Xavier. An officer found him in the housing unit and told him to call me back. He was put on speakerphone in the warden's office, and I broke the news amid cheers and clapping from the staff. His sentence had been reduced from 25 to 18 years, pending the governor's signature.

The signature took weeks, and the wait was agonizing. But once it came, we had seven days left. Seven days until freedom. The official commutation process took over a year from beginning to end—an exhausting year of nerve-wracking uncertainties and sleepless nights.

§

Even though my house was new, having been built less than a year prior, I spent the days leading up to his release meticulously cleaning it as though I had lived in it with an army for half a century. I scrubbed the grout between the tiles on the floor, rubbed away dust from the baseboards, washed the curtains, cleaned under the fridge, made room for him in the closet, and even washed all the windows inside and out. I watered, pruned, and shined the hundreds of plants around the house. The new mattress I bought for us to share as a couple was adorned with bright yellow linens and matching pillow covers. I touched up spots on the walls that needed fresh paint, and I washed every piece of laundry in the house. The whole place sparkled.

Xavier's release was set for 7 a.m. on a Friday in August, but I arrived at the prison early. When I stopped at the officer's booth, I told Officer Martinez that this would be my final trip.

"He's coming home today!" I exclaimed.

Officer Martinez gave me a thumbs-up and an enormous smile. "Oh, yeah? That's great. Xavier, right?"

"Yup." I was elated.

He waved me in, and I sped to the corner parking spot closest to the walkway. When I parked, I walked up the hill to the visiting room area. On that day, Officer Scowl worked at the front desk. She was the least friendly of all the people I had encountered there. Her attitude and demeanor reminded me of my former colleagues at the Annex. She was condescendingly rude to visitors, and her tone was always short.

"Are you here for a family visit?" she said sharply.

"Um, no, I'm here to pick up my husband. He is being released today," I bragged humbly.

"Wait for him in the parking lot, not in here." She turned back to the papers on the massive wraparound counter before her.

I gave her an icy stare and then exited. Standing outside the building I had entered as a visitor and volunteer many times, I turned my camera upward and began snapping pictures. I had hoped to create a scrapbook of his first day out of prison, but she stepped out the side door and bellowed, "Is that a camera? You can't take pictures on prison grounds." She stood motionless with one hand on her hip and one foot propped open the door until I walked away.

As I gained traction on my walk, Ms. Suite popped out from that same side door. "I'll wait with you." Ms. Suite was an office worker who had been nice to me. She wore the same golden t-shirt every time I saw her, and she gushed about Xavier's impending release as we walked downhill toward my car. Having seen him at the facility for many years, Ms. Suite passionately believed he was ready for a successful life on the outside.

About 15 minutes passed while we riffed about the blazing sun and our plans for the remainder of the day. We caught sight of the white van coming down the hill into the parking lot. I noticed Xavier in the back seat with two or three other men. The driver pulled in front of my car. I completely lost my composure. Jumping up and down and screaming excitedly, I was electrified that Xavier was free. Joy washed over me as Xavier exited the van and grabbed trash bags and boxes of well-worn books, clothes, papers, and other personal items. His entire life was condensed into those bags and boxes, and they barely fit into the trunk and backseat of my car.

Once in my car, we relished the moment. As we were leaving the parking lot, I handed him a $500 Visa gift card to spend as he pleased, saving him from having to ask. Initially, Xavier felt anxious during the ride. He focused on the yellow lines that divided the two-lane highway as the oncoming traffic unnerved him.

Our first stop was Starbucks. He was thrilled to treat me to coffee with his gift card. Next, we headed to my favorite thrift store in the area, a vast wonderland of gems on the south side of Sacramento. Xavier needed shirts, pants, jackets, running clothes, shoes, and a suit. My gut sank as he threw about five pairs of $20 jeans in the cart. He found two suits and tossed them in the cart without trying on anything. Shoes, shirts, and shorts hung over the cart's edge, and he was on cloud nine. The clothes totaled over $400, the most I had ever spent at a thrift store. I should have admitted that I thought he was going overboard and hoped he would use his gift card to buy the items he picked up. Many of the clothes did not even fit, and he gave them away the following week.

The next stage of our adventure found us in the bustling aisles of a super Walmart, where he filled the cart with a colorful array of food and candy, a pair of giant fuzzy slippers, underwear, school supplies, and a laptop that he described as "cheap" a few months later. We then had lunch with Xavier's former mentor. Finally, we stopped at Best Buy. He wanted the Samsung phone that had just been released that day, so I added him to my plan and showed him how to use it. Our excitement grew as we got closer to Chico. I was eager to show him the home I had created for us.

Finally, we made it home. We pulled into the driveway. Instead of parking in the garage and walking through the laundry room, I wanted him to experience the house through the front door like a gift I was unwrapping for him.

"You're home. What do you think?"

"It's nice." He spent little time exploring because he was dying to go for a run.

Even though he did not say much more than "it's nice," I hoped he would notice the care I had taken to make the house feel like a home. As soon as we entered, he immediately changed into his running clothes and jetted out the front door to run. After he left, I sat in the living room and tuned into the stillness.

§

I took him to brunch on his second day free. He was overly eager to impress my close friend Tracy, whom I'd spoken about often. Though three of my other close friends sat at the table with us, most of his energy went toward Tracy. He knew how much she meant to me, and it felt like he was trying to win her approval by making me the target of his jokes. He disparaged me and laughed while I sat beside him, stone-faced. For much of the meal, his body was turned away from me, leaving me feeling invisible. I wanted my friends to see us as we were at the prison—blissful and affectionate. Instead, he gave them a version of us that felt foreign and cold.

When we got in the car, I told him how much his behavior had hurt me. "Why would you act like that? Making me the brunt of your jokes was demeaning."

"I was just trying to get to know your friends," he said, brushing it off. "What did I do? I was just talking to Tracy. You act like... Never mind."

The rest of the ride was silent. By the time we got home, he changed into his running clothes and went out for a jog. I stayed behind, sitting in the stillness of our house, feeling the distance between us stretch wider. That moment, I would learn much later, was a wound we never quite healed.

§

The following week, Xavier said he wanted a bicycle. We went to a few shops downtown before he settled on a $400 bike, using the rest of the Visa gift card I'd given him and some of his financial aid to buy it. A week later, he exchanged it for a $600 bike. Then he wanted a car, so we visited a dealership. He test-drove the model he'd read about online, and my nerves were on edge as I sat in the passenger seat. It had been almost 20 years since he last drove. The dealer asked for a down payment, and because Xavier's credit was less than stellar, I offered to let him use the tuition money he had promised to reimburse me.

Months later, a coworker of his offered to sell him a motorcycle, and Xavier couldn't resist. He asked me for a $2,800 loan. I agreed and even drove him to pick it up. Following him home in my car, I watched him struggle with the gears, stalling and jerking until traffic piled up behind us. Eventually, he got the hang of it. That motorcycle didn't last long—someone backed into it in a parking lot, and soon after, he went to Harley-Davidson and bought a new one.

§

"Was that okay?" Xavier would often ask after meeting my friends or colleagues. "Did I do okay?" He constantly sought validation. To him, the highest compliment was when someone remarked, "Wow, you don't look or act like someone who was in prison."

Publicly, he loved talking about the governor's commutation of his sentence. He relished the attention, but privately, he pulled away from me. The letters, phone calls, and deep conversations we had when he was incarcerated dwindled into silence. "Silence kept me safe in prison," he'd say when I pressed him. That silence became a wall between us. I once told him, "Your silence will be the reason this marriage fails." He nodded and promised to do better, but change never came.

When I asked if we could discuss household expenses, he said, "There's nothing to discuss. Just tell me how much money to give you." He took on the gas and electricity bills but offered little else. I hoped he'd contribute more—if not financially, then with chores. One day, he surprised me with $250 worth of beef he'd bought from a truck parked at the mall. I thanked him, but what I really needed was his help. He lay in bed scrolling through his phone as I cleaned, painted, and tended to the house. Occasionally, he worked in the yard and posted about it on Facebook, as if he'd done a day's work.

§

At around 3 a.m. one night, I woke to find him lying next to me, entranced by a pornographic film on his phone. I rolled over silently, but the next day, I texted him, asking if he could refrain from watching porn while I slept beside him. We'd watched it together once, but he had been stiff and awkward. Later, he admitted he preferred watching it alone. "It's easier," he said. "I don't have to negotiate how fast or slow to get to the good parts."

I began finding travel-size bottles of lotion next to the toilet and realized he spent extended periods in the bathroom watching porn. Curious, I changed the Wi-Fi settings to block adult sites. Within 24 hours, he confronted me, frustrated that he couldn't log on. "I'm an adult. I can watch what I want," he said, defensive and ashamed.

Months later, I asked, "Is masturbation your preferred form of sexual stimulation?"

"Yeah, I think so," he admitted.

His preference cut deeper than I wanted to admit. I had assumed his habits in prison were a substitute for real intimacy, but they weren't. They were his preference. I took it personally, even though I knew I shouldn't. Once, I asked him to abstain for a few days before one of our conjugal visits. He accused me of shaming him. Looking back, I wonder if I had ignored the warning signs for too long.

§

When the honeymoon phase ends, quirks can morph into irritants. When Xavier stopped holding space for me, things about him that once seemed endearing now grated on me. He always had food clinging to his lips when he ate, oblivious until prompted to wipe it off. At the prison, I had gestured lovingly, but now, with our connection dimmed, watching him eat was a trial. *Do you not feel the food on your face and lips?*

"I gotta poop." His daily announcements never amused me, but as my irritation with him grew, I finally asked him to stop saying it every single time.

Then there was his fixation on his weight. From the beginning, he had been adamant: he would never weigh 200 pounds. Two hundred was the tipping point into failure. He could live with 199, but 200 was too much. This obsession dictated his life. He restricted food and water, ran harder and longer, and stepped on the scale compulsively to make sure he hadn't crossed the line. But his diet was a paradox—

he fueled his body with junk. Sour candies and sodas replaced water, and sweets had a grip on him. Once, he devoured a five-pound tub of Now & Laters in days, leaving only one flavor, which he handed off to Tracy's mom like a trophy. Empty wrappers littered his side of the bed, a graveyard of late-night indulgence.

One night, he brought an entire plate of ribs into the bedroom and plopped down on the bed to eat.

"No, no, no. Please don't eat those ribs in bed," I begged, exasperated.

Despite his late-night binges and the boxes of food he lugged home from work, his weight haunted him. He was 199 pounds when he left prison, but within six months, he tipped the scale at 207. Those eight pounds consumed him.

Running, masturbation, pornography, and gambling took over as we drifted further apart. A week ago, I realized the cons in our marriage outweighed the pros, and the air between us thickened with tension. Gone was the intimacy. Even friendship felt like a relic.

He started coming home later and later, slipping into a casino after work to gamble away the night. Sobriety had been a cornerstone of his redemption arc, but he never mentioned his gambling problem—a habit he had nurtured early in his confinement. He borrowed money from me often and once took out a loan from a sketchy company he'd found through spam mail. In a single month, he withdrew over $5,000 at the casino ATM.

Xavier's workday ended at 9:30 p.m., but two nights in April 2019, he strolled in after 1 a.m. On the third night, it was 4 a.m.

"Where you been?" I asked, groggy and trying not to sound accusatory.

He didn't answer, just set two hundred-dollar bills on my nightstand and lay down on the floor. He hadn't slept in the bed for over a week, claiming the mattress was too soft and hurt his back.

"You aren't attracted to me, are you?" I asked. I had posed this question before, but by now, the answer felt all but obvious. He had never once looked at my body with lust, and whatever attraction he might have had was now imperceptible.

His voice was hesitant, high-pitched. "The extra weight around your waist... It makes it hard to get into certain sex positions."

His response stunned me, not for what he said but for what it revealed. Our sex life had dwindled to rote, infrequent encounters. One position, one script, and I lay there, turned away, waiting for him to finish.

I weighed 236, just one pound more than I was on our wedding day. The gut he now complained about had always been there. Still, I bought a gym membership and ran a few times before losing motivation and stopping altogether. I didn't want to change for him.

Perhaps he had a long-held hope that he would inspire me to join in his obsession to run and lose weight. He once told me he would create an exercise regimen I could do in the hot tub.

"See, look. You can do these easily." He leaned onto the side of the tub and did five standing pushups while I stood on the patio with my arms crossed. I never asked him to create any workout plans for me. He enjoyed exercising in the hot tub, which drove me crazy since he sweats excessively. He always messed up the chemical makeup of the water, and he never purchased new chemicals or cleaned the tub. Besides, I do not think he genuinely cared for my health as much as he wanted an exercise partner. Perhaps he was not attracted to my body, which is fine. At the very least, I had hoped he would find my body an un-issue, as I had done with the acute alopecia that left him with no eyebrows, a bald head, and splotchy skin.

§

We argued through text the day after his response to my question had me all in my feelings. As usual, he got off work at 9:30 p.m. This time, he chose not to come home at all. I had gotten used to him coming in later and later, but he had never stayed out the entire night before. I grew frustrated as the hours passed. He rejected all my calls. My text messages went unanswered. I became increasingly anxious as the night wore on. In addition to expressing for months how his choice to go running instead of talking impacted our relationship, I explained how much I hated being ignored. Around 2:30 a.m., he turned off his phone altogether, and all my calls went straight to voicemail. At first, I just hung up, but then I began to leave messages.

"You're making this worse by ignoring me." "Call me back."

Worried, anxious, and enraged, I hopped in my car and drove around town, looking for him. I snaked through the streets, went to his job on the other side of town, and rolled through the casino's parking lot, where I often saw his car. I circled the university, unsure of what I would have said if I had found him. I decided to go back home.

By 6 a.m., I was seething. I yanked a handful of large black trash bags from under the kitchen cabinet, and, like a tornado raging through an open field, I threw his belongings into those bags. His school papers, photos, shoes, and underwear were tossed into one bag after another. I wanted all his shit gone. I was on a mission to rid my house of every trace of him, especially the avalanche of letters in which he addressed me as "Sweets." As the minutes ticked away without his response, I became more aggressive. His boxes and bags, which still carried the stench of prison, were strewn around my garage. They were not spared; I sent them skidding toward the garage door with a swift kick. Clearing the onslaught of trash on his side of the bed, including candy wrappers and torn paper, was detoxifying. I then purged all the photos of us from my phone.

At about 6:20 a.m., I texted him that the door code had been changed, his belongings had been packed, and his presence in my house was no longer welcome. I had reached my breaking point. I was unshackled, but I was not free. The taste of the end was bitter.

He rang the doorbell at about 8:15 a.m. and began loading his car. I did not know where he had been and did not care to ask. Even now, his whereabouts during those hours remain a mystery. I am unsure where he stayed for the next day or two, but he eventually rented someone's converted garage space.

I felt deep remorse for how things ended. We began texting and chatting a bit. He repeatedly told me how embarrassed he was that I put him out. I apologized profusely and said I might have handled it differently if I had it to do over again. He said he did not trust me anymore, so I apologized again. He told me he would never forgive me. I continued apologizing, but then I reminded myself that he responded to an argument by staying out all night without a warning, explanation, or apology. Nothing. I reminded myself that his behavior was a final "fuck you" to me, so at some point, I stopped saying I was sorry. Indeed, he could not have thought there would be business as usual after he ignored me all night. He was ready for the relationship to be over, too.

Still, weeks later, he texted, asking if we could try again. I said no.

§

The sting came later when I saw my last name still attached to his on Facebook—right next to a photo of him with his new girlfriend. Xavier had been at my house just a week before, returning borrowed money. He hadn't mentioned her once. We'd spoken frequently in the 58 days since our split. He'd even gone with me to put down my two-year-old cat and worked on a bathroom project I'd paid him for just ten days before.

"You could have at least told me you were seeing someone," I texted after a mutual friend alerted me to the post.

"Sorry," he replied.

And just like that, he became *X*. The man I loved ceased to exist. That's the name I still use whenever I talk about him.

I was not jealous about his new relationship, but I kept ruminating on the belief that he would show up for her in ways he did not for me. He would choose words instead of silence with her. He would never belittle her in front of her friends. He would accept her body just as it is.

After X unfriended and blocked me on Facebook, my brother sent him a biting text message accusing him of using me as a steppingstone to get out of prison. Despite X and I not speaking, X sent me a screenshot of my brother's message.

"Is this what we're doing now?"

"Just ignore him like you ignore me," I shot back.

"I will."

A few weeks after my brother's message, I sent him my own rant about how he did not live up to the promises he made.

He replied, "I don't need you. I never needed you."

I never accused him of needing me, and I never aspired to be needed. I wanted to be cherished, accepted, and held close to his heart. I did not want his dependence. I craved a mutual bond where I could be loved, seen, and heard.

His words stung, not because I wanted to be needed, but because they erased everything I had done for him. Nobody else had carved the pathway that led him out of prison. Nobody else had been there when he was released. Thus, his text about not needing me would have been struck with searing honesty had he dared to include the word "anymore." He did not need me—anymore. And it's that distinction that clarifies why his investment in our marriage changed.

"I had somewhere else I could have gone." He was referring to an invitation extended by an older woman who volunteered at the prison the day I watched him run 23 laps. She offered to allow him to stay in the guest house on her property if he was ever released. I am sure she is a kind-hearted, lovely person. But she did not call the governor, bug the commutation board, or do anything else to help him get free. Still, I never threw anything up in his face about all I had done for him.

The story he tells now—and I know I shouldn't care—is that his good behavior as a model prisoner earned him his freedom. And yes, that was part of it. Across this country, countless incarcerated individuals have turned their lives around, becoming role models of reform. But redemption alone doesn't open the gates. Prison officials don't sift through files, looking for stories of transformation to celebrate. The heavy lifting happens on the outside, in phone calls, petitions, and relentless advocacy. I don't want to undermine his achievements; he made incredible strides. But X wouldn't be riding his Harley through the streets of a town I've called home for 24 years without the tireless work I put into securing his release.

Karen checked on me often after things fell apart. She knew how deeply I had invested in this marriage. When X unfriended her on social media, it was as if Karen's years of support had suddenly lost their value. X didn't need her *anymore*, either.

§

Bitterness gnawed at me. I turned the rage inward because I had made similar mistakes before. I spent months revisiting every choice, every sacrifice, every sign I ignored. Shame and sadness swelled, so heavily they dulled my will to live. My thoughts became muddy and chaotic, whispering escape as the only way to silence the relentless weight of it all. The idea of disappearing felt like relief.

Even therapy couldn't pull me from the quicksand. I often had sessions on the side of the road, gripping the wheel, struggling to keep it together. Kimberlee, my mom, Tracy, and my aunt were lifelines I clung to, but I was still drowning. Living was hard. Trusting was hard. Being alone was hard. Looking at myself in the mirror was hard. But nothing was harder than losing the first 200 pounds. I put that on God.

I didn't want X back. That was clear. But somewhere deep inside, a part of me wanted to prove something to him, to myself, to everyone who thought I wouldn't recover. So, I started walking. First, it was just steps. Then, brisk jogs. I parked a mile away from campus and walked in every day, sometimes with a determined stride, sometimes running. I tried intermittent fasting, eating in a six-hour window and drinking only water for 18 hours. With each day, I gained strength and confidence. I treated myself to running gear, new sneakers, and a smartwatch to track my progress. In six months, I shed nearly 50 pounds and ran two 5k races in the same month.

I saw him at the starting line of my first race. Although we didn't exchange glances, I was exhilarated during the run, confident that he noticed me and saw that I was thinner. The following day, I reached out to Paul for confirmation. He had been the best man at our wedding and was recently released after nearly four decades of custody.

Paul hesitated. "He didn't mention anything." My chest tightened with humiliation. Why was I still seeking approval from someone who had drained me of so much? Why was I still tethered to his ghost, craving acknowledgment of my effort, my transformation? I realized I had spent a lifetime learning that love and kindness had to be earned. If others didn't reciprocate, I saw it as a failure in me. X and I were alike in that way, but it didn't soften the blow.

The next day, I called Paul again, this time to apologize. That conversation marked the beginning of my own release.

§

I should have asked myself the hard questions from the start. Why did I think I was suited for a relationship like this? Why did I seek love from someone whose very presence in my life demanded so much sacrifice? What in me thought this was the best I could do? I ignored the red flags, told myself I could fix the cracks if I worked hard enough, poured enough love into the spaces between us. I clung to his fleeting tenderness, his promises, even when his actions painted a different truth.

If one day you ever have a change of heart, please don't hurt her.

§

Toward the end of our relationship, X accused me of changing from the person I was when I visited him in prison. Maybe I had. The biggest shift in my life was when he moved into my home. My professional life, circle of friends, finances, and daily routine remained intact. It was his entire world that had turned upside down. Still, I admit I coped with his hurtful behavior during his incarceration by shrinking myself and prioritizing his needs. Even after months of him being home, I was still being pushed aside. That's when I decided to prioritize my safety and express my thoughts and feelings. I suspect doing so reminded him of the women in his past, especially his mother, who refused to tolerate his selfish, hurtful behavior.

In that sense, yes, I had changed.

§

Behind the hearty laughter and the clinical terms, he swishes around his mouth, X is an arrogant imposter. My relationship with him often felt reminiscent of engaging in "the shell game," where a performer uses three shells and a ball in a complex interplay of misdirection, speed, manipulation, and skill. Diversion tactics confuse the audience about the ball's location, and the rapid changes in our relationship were akin to the swift movements in the shell game, which often left me deciphering his emotions and true intentions. Just as in my marriage, when the smooth operator lets players occasionally win to instill false confidence, X occasionally conceded with silence and made temporary behavioral changes, which fostered a false sense of security and progress.

I believed my eyes were wide open when, in reality, I had no idea what had happened until he showed me the ball under a fourth shell. A few months after the breakup, he texted, "That first time you got mad at me for laughing with Tracy at brunch set the stage for our entire relationship." Are you kidding me? That happened less than 24 hours after I picked him up from prison. Why was I learning this now, almost a year later? My reaction to his behavior wasn't an explosion. It was sadness and a calm, empowering statement about how his jokes made me feel demeaned and invisible. I didn't yell. I didn't berate him. Yet somehow, this was the defining moment of our marriage?

For eight months, I fought an uphill battle, trying to build something meaningful. The years of waking at dawn to drive to see him didn't "set the stage"? Not the running shoes I ensured he had or the love I poured into his case before the parole board? If he wanted to reduce everything to that moment at brunch, I was willing to revisit it too. He sat at a table with my closest friends, laughing at my expense, and when I told him how it hurt me, his response was to go silent and run. And he kept running for eight months until I finally decided I'd had enough.

I responded to his text, saying, "You've never allowed yourself to be vulnerable with me."

His succinct and striking reply was, "I haven't allowed myself to be vulnerable with anyone." I grappled with a mix of emotions: regret, frustration, and rage. It was a painful realization that I fell in love with a man who was an impenetrable fortress.

I was distraught, wishing I could rip my brain out through my ears. I thought obsessively about what I felt he owed me: the same kindness, loyalty, and commitment I showed him. I felt betrayed by how easily he walked away from me—from us—months before I put him out.

He simply stopped showing up. He stopped using his words. He stopped holding space for me. I sacrificed a lot, and he promised God and my mama that he would never break my heart. Once he decided he didn't care anymore, he should have said so. I suspect he said nothing because he had no money to move out.

§

Amid the fog one afternoon, I desperately needed human contact. I journeyed to the mall to drop in on the massage spot that offers fifteen-minute back rubs for $12. When I arrived, the only attendant on duty was a young man of about 22 who had beaten my back so hard the month before that he left me in pain for more than a week. I hate it when even the gentlest masseuses bang on my back at the end of the massage, and this dude messed me up pretty badly. The second I saw him, I zipped past the massage chairs and strolled from the east end of the mall to the west, sobbing.

My good girlfriend, Tracy, messaged and asked a question we commonly ask each other: What you doing?

I typed, "I'm done." She weathered the breakup with me and rightly assumed what I meant.

Sensing the gravity of my message, she promptly called me. "Where are you?" Her voice was thick and penetrating.

"I'm at the mall," I said with a crack in my throat.

"Go stand outside. I'll be right there."

Feeling as if everyone in the mall was walking in one direction while I walked alone in the opposite direction, I eventually made it outside of JCPenney. Sadness consumed me while I leaned on the edge of the wall—on the edge of myself.

He had positioned himself as second in my life, behind my mom and before Tracy, whom he called "Number Three." But it was Number Three who came to save me. Soon, she pulled up and took me out of town for an upscale dinner.

§

I had poured my soul into our relationship, trusting him completely and believing he would show me the same level of care I showed him. Instead, he ignored me, offered nothing to the household, and borrowed money too often. But nothing hurt more than the fact that he had stopped using words.

When I severed the relationship, he spoke plenty. Whispers of his words, passed on by mutual friends, my students, and other people we knew, filtered back to me. He said I kicked him out because I am a mean person. He also told people I encouraged folks at the university to alienate him, which was true only in his head. The "proof" was when he said hello to my friend Tray on campus, and Tray did not say hello back. When I asked him, Tray said he hadn't even seen X on campus that day. Even if he had ignored him (which Tray would never do), X did not understand that he was never entitled to my friends. Their acceptance of him was always contingent upon his kindness and connection to me.

My friends heard me gush over X for a couple of years, but they were not incredibly impressed with how he treated me at brunch on his second day home—nor any other day after that. Contrary to what he believes, I did not suggest to anyone how they should treat him, and no one I know has ever engaged him rudely or disrespectfully or spread negative information about him. But X needed to be seen as "good," especially by people with influence. He craved validation, yet he couldn't see how his actions alienated him. The narrative he spun was his way of justifying a truth he wasn't ready to face: feeling discarded is a hell of a sensation.

§

Recently, I saw a TikTok that hit the nail on the head for me. The brother said the following words:

"You can be a whole package, and I mean a whole one, but if you end up at the wrong address, the receiver will mishandle you. Misplaced people will have us second-guessing ourselves, thinking we're asking for too much because they can't offer much. Could the problem be that you're seeking validation from someone who is not even valid for your destiny? So now you have heartache because you keep misplacing people. Pain prevention is tied to people being properly placed."

Ha'mercy. When I tell you this hit me like a brick—whew! I cannot explain how much this resonated. I don't know if hearing those words before meeting Xavier would have changed anything, but they have made everything clear now.

I leaned into Lise, my therapist, who helped me navigate my way back to myself. She gave me strategies to forgive myself and reminded me of who I was before X entered my life. I was *Nandi*, a name rooted in South African tradition, meaning "woman of high esteem." She validated my well-honed communication skills and pointed out that X's inability to hold space for me wasn't a failure on my part.

"It's not that he won't," she said. "He can't. He doesn't

have the skills."

But he used to, I argued. He used to.

Whether he couldn't or wouldn't didn't matter anymore.

§

In my darkest moments, I sought solace in the hauntingly beautiful strains of Jazmine Sullivan's "Forever Don't Last," a nine-minute catharsis set in a smoky theater with deep blue lights. Jazmine's voice blends seamlessly with the soulful tones of an organ, weaving a rich gospel melody. The painful reality was echoed in her refrain, "Forever doesn't last too long these days."

As the song reaches its crescendo, the bass reverberates. Then comes the moment when Jazmine breaks down the word "miserable" into individual syllables. The song is a devastating portrayal of the misery accompanying a shattered heart. The rawness in her delivery was devastating, but it was the line *"Lord knows I gave it my all"* that shattered me.

I played that performance on repeat, each viewing carving a path toward acceptance. When Jazmine turned the mic to the audience, inviting them to sing along—*" Trying don't work, so I just have to face that forever doesn't last too long"*—I felt the chorus of shared pain wrap around me. She reminded me I wasn't alone. Somewhere in the world, someone else knew the weight of a love that couldn't hold.

That song became my companion—in my home, in the car, in my headphones. Jazmine's voice pushed me toward a new chapter. The conditioning that once bound me—that love was transactional, that kindness must always be earned—began to unravel.

Every tear, every note, every ache in my chest was part of a journey toward self-love and the pursuit of a forever that *would* last.

§

I wanted my name back.

When I asked about filing for a no-contest divorce, a courthouse employee said it could be finalized instantly since X and I had no joint property, finances, or children. I sent X a string of urgent texts, asking him to meet me at the courthouse to sign the papers. I included the cost and asked him to split it with me. He ignored me for more than a month before finally agreeing.

In the courthouse lobby, we avoided eye contact. He perched on a windowsill, holding his phone to his ear as if mid-conversation, though I don't believe anyone was on the line. When our number was called, we approached the clerk's window. He asked to borrow money to cover his half.

Reluctantly, I handed it over. That $215—money I knew I'd never see again—felt like a bargain for reclaiming my name. Of course, he didn't pay me back.

The clerk's initial claim that the divorce could be finalized instantly turned out to be wrong. In California, it takes six months and one day.

After signing the papers, I stepped into the parking lot, tilted my head to the sky, and whispered a heartfelt prayer: *Thank you, Lawd.* Gratitude swelled within me—for the strength to walk this road and the wisdom to have created a prenuptial agreement. That document ensured my home and finances remained mine. Thank. You. Lawd.

On January 2, 2020, the official day of my divorce, jubilation surged through me. The end of that challenging chapter had arrived, and the day marked the definitive closure of a tumultuous journey.

§

X was every prisoner I once loved, all rolled into one. He was one big ball of every relationship I have ever had with prisoners, especially those where we shared an abundance of beautiful words before we fell silent.

There would have been no Xavier without nadir, Halim, J, Saad, Shawn, Keith, Justin, Reggie, or Joe. He embodied the one-sided nature of those connections, which I expected would become more balanced once a person was free. He embodied the most generous and the most desperate ways I showed up to love, driven by a belief in redemption, vulnerability, and mutual respect. Without my previous experiences—the pen pals, my cousin, my work as a correctional officer, and all my volunteer work—I would never have trusted him or myself enough to love a prisoner again.

§

About three years after our breakup, X texted me from an unknown number.

"Who is this?" I could not have imagined it.

"It's Xavier." He wrote that he had some prison-related work I might want to participate in. I deleted the message and blocked his number without responding.

§

If I could talk to partners who show up year after year to prisons all over the country, holding onto hope for a good life on the outside with their incarcerated loved ones—especially those they didn't know before incarceration—I'd tell them this:

- The first day out of prison marks a new beginning, not just for them but for your relationship.

- They will go through a rediscovery process, and that may shift who they are.
- They've developed habits, fears, and traumas that served them in prison but can become destructive in freedom. Silence, for example, might have been lifesaving inside but can become a barrier outside.
- Unless they consciously recognize and address how prison has changed them, they may continue to rely on survival strategies that make no sense in your relationship.
- Your love will not fix them.
- Center yourself. Prioritize your own emotional well-being. Full stop.

§

I started wearing my wedding ring again recently. It's a stunning, custom-made piece of art by an African American jeweler—a white-gold band with ten diamonds cascading down each side, crowned with a cowrie shell. Cowrie shells were once a powerful currency, and legend says wearing them grants sacred goddess protection.

When I first saw the ring, I couldn't stop gushing about it. X insisted I buy it, promising to repay me the $1900 once he was free and working. That never happened, and I never asked. For two years after our breakup, the ring sat tucked away in a jewelry box behind my closet door.

On my birthday in 2022, I took it to a local jeweler and had it resized to fit a finger on my right hand. When I look at the ring now, I no longer see the shadow of his broken promises. I no longer feel the ache of what it once meant. Instead, it glimmers as a testament to my resilience—a masterpiece born of pain and self-reclamation. The cowrie shell on top, once currency, now reminds me that I am of immeasurable worth. This ring, with its cascade of diamonds, is no longer tied to him. It is tied to me—to the woman who picked herself up from the wreckage and chose to invest in her own brilliance.

§

Three days before my divorce was final, I went on what I hope will be my last first date. Filled with excitement and uncertainty, I was unsure whether I truly knew how to be vulnerable again. But the butterflies in my belly propelled me forward, urging me to embrace the new wave and see where it would lead me.

As of this writing, I have been madly in love with LaMichael for five years. We had only been dating for three months when he packed a bag to shelter in place with me after the governor shut everything down due to COVID. We were in each other's company almost 24/7 from March to September 2020, when he returned to work. Since then, we have lived together, traveled the country, and fallen asleep holding hands practically every night. We were married in a beautiful ceremony on June 22, 2024.

We've never argued or felt tension. Not once. We've never ignored each other, made jokes at each other's expense, stormed off, slammed a door, rolled an eye, or checked out. We give each other tenderness in abundance. With him, I feel secure—100% of the time.

I told Tracy that getting along with LaMichael was one of the easiest things I had ever done. She affirmed, "Nandi, you are easy to get along with, too. That's who you are when you feel safe." Tracy also makes me feel safe, and I express tenderness with her, too.

§

After X left, I swapped out the mattress I'd bought for us with one from my Airbnb. When LaMichael and I committed to a life filled with love and tenderness, he helped me load that "marital bed" into a van and take it to the dump. Heaving it into the pile was a cathartic act of release, a final cleansing. Afterward, I bought a new one for us—a fresh start.

Despite LaMichael being an incredible chef, I now weigh 90 pounds less than the day I married X. It took until I was 50 years old and committed to this beautiful human before I learned that pleasure is intentional and happens only when I feel safe. Nothing is complicated about that or about loving him. And he has never once struggled to love me back.

I also have a new motorcycle now. When we ride together, sharing the lane, the wind rushes past, and the open road stretches before me, I feel my own independence humming in the engine.

I'm moving forward. Freedom.

I'm free.

ABOUT THE AUTHOR

Dr. Nandi Sojourner Crosby, affectionately known to her students as "Dr. Nandi," is more than a professor—she is a storyteller, a fierce advocate for social justice, and a believer in second chances. For over two decades, she has taught sociology at California State University, Chico, and Butte College, igniting conversations about social inequality, mass incarceration, and the many invisible walls that divide us. From 2015 to 2018, she brought her classroom into the walls of a prison through the Incarcerated Students Program with Feather River College, an experience that deepened her understanding of the human stories behind the statistics.

But Dr. Nandi's connection to the prison system began long before that. Raised in Baltimore, Maryland, she once walked the cold, echoing corridors of a maximum-security men's prison as a correctional officer—a role that forced her to confront the harsh realities of the criminal justice system. That experience didn't harden her; it cracked her open. It sparked a passion to challenge the systems that cage people physically and mentally. Her life's work has been about dismantling those cages—one conversation, one story, one student at a time.

Her unwavering commitment to incarcerated and formerly incarcerated people runs deep. Dr. Nandi doesn't just research or teach about prison life—she has sat with it, befriended it, and carried its stories in her heart. Through volunteer work, mentorship, and advocacy, she has spent decades amplifying voices that society would rather silence.

Dr. Nandi holds a B.A. in Psychology from St. Mary's College of Maryland, an M.A. in Africana Women's Studies from Clark Atlanta University—where she first fell in love with Black feminist thought—and a Ph.D. in Sociology from Georgia State University. In 2016, she was honored as Chico State's Outstanding Teacher of the Year, though her true reward has always been found in the growth and curiosity of her students.

Driven by the belief that stories can heal and disrupt, Dr. Nandi founded FreedomConscious Ink, a private press that amplifies the voices of incarcerated men and women. Through nonfiction essays and biographies, FreedomConscious Ink brings forward stories of struggle and triumph, inviting readers to look beyond judgment and into the humanity of those entangled in the prison system. Its mission is simple yet radical: challenge society's perceptions, foster empathy, and create space for restorative justice and second chances.

Dr. Nandi believes fiercely in the potential for

redemption. She advocates for a society that meets returning citizens with opportunities instead of obstacles. Her work bridges theory and lived experience—examining the systemic roots of mass incarceration while actively working toward dismantling them. She knows real change comes not just from policy shifts but from hearts and minds opening.

Whether speaking to a crowded auditorium, guiding a classroom discussion, or sitting face-to-face with someone who has known nothing but steel and concrete, Dr. Nandi meets people where they are—with honesty, compassion, and unwavering belief in their worth.

When she isn't teaching or writing, Dr. Nandi finds joy in the simple things—tending to her indoor garden, crafting, redecorating corners of her home, hunting for treasures in thrift stores, and chasing new adventures around the globe. Someday, she plans to let her humor take center stage with a comedy book titled *Made-Up Tales of Thrift Store Wedding Dresses*.

Through every facet of her work, Dr. Nandi Sojourner Crosby remains a force for change—a woman who listens deeply, loves boldly, and believes in the power of stories to heal and transform.